The World Trade Organization

DATE DUE

OPPOSING
VIEWPOINTS®
SERIES

The World
Trade Organization

Other Books of Related Interest:

Opposing Viewpoints Series

Globalization

Free Trade

Social Justice

At Issue Series

Is There a New Cold War?

What Is the Future of the U.S. Economy?

Current Controversies Series

Fair Trade

The World Economy

"Congress shall make
no law . . . abridging
the freedom of speech,
or of the press."

First Amendment to the U.S. Constitution

The basic foundation of our democracy is the First Amendment guarantee of freedom of expression. The Opposing Viewpoints Series is dedicated to the concept of this basic freedom and the idea that it is more important to practice it than to enshrine it.

OPPOSING VIEWPOINTS® SERIES

The World Trade Organization

Margaret Haerens, Book Editor

GREENHAVEN PRESS
A part of Gale, Cengage Learning

 GALE
CENGAGE Learning™

Detroit • New York • San Francisco • New Haven, Conn • Waterville, Maine • London

Christine Nasso, *Publisher*
Elizabeth Des Chenes, *Managing Editor*

© 2010 Greenhaven Press, a part of Gale, Cengage Learning

Gale and Greenhaven Press are registered trademarks used herein under license.

For more information, contact:
Greenhaven Press
27500 Drake Rd.
Farmington Hills, MI 48331-3535
Or you can visit our Internet site at gale.cengage.com

Articles in Greenhaven Press anthologies are often edited for length to meet page requirements. In addition, original titles of these works are changed to clearly present the main thesis and to explicitly indicate the author's opinion. Every effort is made to ensure that Greenhaven Press accurately reflects the original intent of the authors. Every effort has been made to trace the owners of copyrighted material.

Cover image © Scott Picunko/Images.com/Corbis

LIBRARY OF CONGRESS CATALOGING-IN-PUBLICATION DATA

The World Trade Organization / Margaret Haerens, Book Editor.
    p. cm. -- (Opposing viewpoints)
    Includes bibliographical references and index.
    ISBN 978-0-7377-4785-0 (hardcover) -- ISBN 978-0-7377-4786-7 (pbk.)
    1. World Trade Organization. 2. United States--Foreign economic relations. 3. United States--Economic policy. I. Haerens, Margaret.
    HF1385.W6663 2010
    382'.92--dc22
                                            2009052257

Printed in the United States of America
1 2 3 4 5 6 7 14 13 12 11 10

Contents

Chapter 4: How Should the United States Relate to the WTO?

Why Consider Opposing Viewpoints?

> *"The only way in which a human being can make some approach to knowing the whole of a subject is by hearing what can be said about it by persons of every variety of opinion and studying all modes in which it can be looked at by every character of mind. No wise man ever acquired his wisdom in any mode but this."*
>
> *John Stuart Mill*

In our media-intensive culture it is not difficult to find differing opinions. Thousands of newspapers and magazines and dozens of radio and television talk shows resound with differing points of view. The difficulty lies in deciding which opinion to agree with and which "experts" seem the most credible. The more inundated we become with differing opinions and claims, the more essential it is to hone critical reading and thinking skills to evaluate these ideas. Opposing Viewpoints books address this problem directly by presenting stimulating debates that can be used to enhance and teach these skills. The varied opinions contained in each book examine many different aspects of a single issue. While examining these conveniently edited opposing views, readers can develop critical thinking skills such as the ability to compare and contrast authors' credibility, facts, argumentation styles, use of persuasive techniques, and other stylistic tools. In short, the Opposing Viewpoints Series is an ideal way to attain the higher-level thinking and reading skills so essential in a culture of diverse and contradictory opinions.

In addition to providing a tool for critical thinking, Opposing Viewpoints books challenge readers to question their own strongly held opinions and assumptions. Most people form their opinions on the basis of upbringing, peer pressure, and personal, cultural, or professional bias. By reading carefully balanced opposing views, readers must directly confront new ideas as well as the opinions of those with whom they disagree. This is not to simplistically argue that everyone who reads opposing views will—or should—change his or her opinion. Instead, the series enhances readers' understanding of their own views by encouraging confrontation with opposing ideas. Careful examination of others' views can lead to the readers' understanding of the logical inconsistencies in their own opinions, perspective on why they hold an opinion, and the consideration of the possibility that their opinion requires further evaluation.

Evaluating Other Opinions

To ensure that this type of examination occurs, Opposing Viewpoints books present all types of opinions. Prominent spokespeople on different sides of each issue as well as well-known professionals from many disciplines challenge the reader. An additional goal of the series is to provide a forum for other, less known, or even unpopular viewpoints. The opinion of an ordinary person who has had to make the decision to cut off life support from a terminally ill relative, for example, may be just as valuable and provide just as much insight as a medical ethicist's professional opinion. The editors have two additional purposes in including these less known views. One, the editors encourage readers to respect others' opinions—even when not enhanced by professional credibility. It is only by reading or listening to and objectively evaluating others' ideas that one can determine whether they are worthy of consideration. Two, the inclusion of such viewpoints encourages the important critical thinking skill of objectively evaluating an author's credentials and bias. This evaluation will illuminate an author's reasons for taking a particular stance on an issue and will aid in readers' evaluation of the author's ideas.

It is our hope that these books will give readers a deeper understanding of the issues debated and an appreciation of the complexity of even seemingly simple issues when good and honest people disagree. This awareness is particularly important in a democratic society such as ours in which people enter into public debate to determine the common good. Those with whom one disagrees should not be regarded as enemies but rather as people whose views deserve careful examination and may shed light on one's own.

Thomas Jefferson once said that "difference of opinion leads to inquiry, and inquiry to truth." Jefferson, a broadly educated man, argued that "if a nation expects to be ignorant and free . . . it expects what never was and never will be." As individuals and as a nation, it is imperative that we consider the opinions of others and examine them with skill and discernment. The Opposing Viewpoints Series is intended to help readers achieve this goal.

David L. Bender and Bruno Leone,
Founders

Introduction

"We are living in a time of crisis. Its full social impact is still to come and it will inevitably create political pressures. And it is precisely now, when protectionist temptations abound, that the value of the multilateral trading system is all the more apparent to us."

—Pascal Lamy,
Director General of
the World Trade Organization

On November 30, 1999, the World Trade Organization (WTO) launched its latest round of trade negotiations, known as "The Millennial Round," at the Washington State Convention and Trade Center in Seattle, Washington. Over a three-day period, member nations were expected to discuss a number of issues, including an important agricultural treaty. However, the much-anticipated negotiations were decisively overshadowed by a series of massive street protests and demonstrations, organized for months by a loose coalition of local, national, and international groups united by their opposition to economic globalization. As these antiglobalization groups marched through the streets of Seattle—estimated to be nearly fifty thousand strong at some points—the demonstration erupted into violence and became a controversial and eye-opening encounter for both the pro-globalization forces and antiglobalization groups.

Globalization refers to the integration of national economies into the international economy through free trade, unfettered migration and flow of capital, foreign direct investment, and the spread of technology. The WTO is an international organization that facilitates economic globalization through a number of measures, including complex free-trade treaties and the resolution of trade disputes. The antiglobalization movement opposes the spread of capitalism in the form of large, multinational organizations that utilize large, multinational trade treaties and deregulated markets to pursue massive profits at the expense of organized labor, the environment, and the people in developing countries. They advocate for more effectual forms of global integration that benefit everyone by focusing on democratic representation, more economic opportunities for impoverished and developing regions, food security, and improved human rights for all people. For the antiglobalization movement, the WTO was one of the obvious international organizations to target and protest, with the goal of disrupting the Millennial Round of trade negotiations in Seattle.

Antiglobalization groups, which included unions, nongovernmental organizations (NGOs), student groups, anarchists, and social justice groups, began organizing for the "Battle of Seattle" months before the WTO meetings. Some groups, like the labor unions umbrella organization AFL-CIO, were motivated by pro-labor interests; others by environmental agendas. Others took a more radical view, opposing capitalism and free trade and advocating a course of civil disobedience during the protests; these groups targeted multinational and chain businesses downtown, such as Starbucks, NikeTown, and Fidelity Investments, whom they felt exploited third-world countries, labor, or the environment. Others, like the Direct Action Network (DAN) aimed to disrupt the WTO talks by blocking streets and intersections in downtown Seattle to block delegates from moving freely to the Convention and Trade Center.

On November 30, alarmed at the growing number of protesters, Seattle police fired pepper spray, tear gas canisters, stun grenades, and rubber bullets at protesters in order to disperse them and reopen the streets. Some protesters began smashing windows and vandalizing storefronts. As the clashes between protesters and police grew more heated, dumpsters were lit on fire, police cars were vandalized, and more property damaged.

More than six hundred protesters were arrested that day. The opening of WTO trade meetings were postponed as police dealt with protesters and cleared the streets. When the negotiations finally commenced after the delay, talks quickly collapsed over disagreements on agricultural policy. For WTO member states, the Millennial Round was a failure.

For many involved in the antiglobalization movement, however, the "Battle in Seattle" was considered a rousing success. The worldwide attention given to the Seattle protests generated massive publicity on the issue of globalization and the growing opposition movement to it. Many people in America had never even considered the consequences of international trade on labor, environment, and third-world countries, and coverage of the Seattle events inspired a number of people to learn about the antiglobalization movement. Globalization became a hot-button issue for a number of Americans on all sides of the political and economic spectrum, particularly as the outsourcing of U.S. jobs became a political issue in the 2004 and 2008 U.S. presidential elections.

As the next round of trade negotiations convened in Doha, Qatar, in 2001, the WTO decided to focus on providing more opportunities for developing countries to create beneficial trade relationships on the world market by lowering trade barriers and other restrictions with developed countries. This round of trade negotiations, known as the Doha Development Round, broke down in 2008 over the issue of agricultural tariffs. WTO officials report that they are very much committed to an economic globalization that benefits both developing and developed countries.

The issues that inspired protesters in Seattle in 1999 are still pertinent today. As the antiglobalization movement has grown, scholars and commentators debate the impact of economic globalization and the spread of capitalism around the world. They question the idea of giving so much power to transnational corporations and international organizations that do not have the interests of labor, the environment, and the poor and exploited in mind. They charge that too much power is concentrated in the hands of multinational businesses that care only about profit and not people and the world around them. The collapse of the Doha Development Round, which aimed to help developing countries compete in the world marketplace, only exacerbates the concerns of those on both sides of the heated issue of economic globalization.

The authors of the viewpoints presented in *Opposing Viewpoints: The World Trade Organization* debate the role and impact of the WTO in the following chapters: What Is the Role of the WTO? Is the WTO Essential to U.S. Interests? How Can the WTO Improve? How Should the United States Relate to the WTO? The information provided in this volume will provide insight into why the WTO has aroused so much controversy as well as the potential benefits of and concern over existing and potential WTO practices and policies.

CHAPTER 1

What Is the Role of the World Trade Organization (WTO)?

Chapter Preface

In 2007 American pet owners became very concerned after a sudden increase of seriously ill dogs and cats was reported by the media. Further investigation traced the outbreak to pet food made from imported animal fodder from China. After lab analysis, it was found that the animal fodder was contaminated with a large concentration of melamine, a chemical compound used by Chinese manufacturers in wheat gluten as a protein substitute. Alarmed U.S. pet food manufacturers pulled the tainted pet food off shelves, but not after a significant number of dogs and cats were adversely affected—some pets even died from the contaminated food.

Further concerns were generated when investigators discovered that a rice protein from China was found to be contaminated with melamine. Then hogs and chickens meant for human consumption were discovered to have been fed with melamine-infused food. In light of the growing China import scandal, the Food and Drug Administration (FDA) was forced to reassure an alarmed public who could not trust the safety of the food found on supermarket shelves.

The melamine scare of 2007–2008 illuminates the dangers of allowing a country with unregulated markets to become the world's largest producer of many foodstuffs. As the U.S. relies more and more on cheap food products made in China and other unregulated countries, the danger of tainted foodstuffs becomes a reality for the American consumer. Because the FDA cannot inspect every product that comes into the United States, many commentators view the World Trade Organization (WTO) as the most plausible international organization to take on the responsibility of establishing global food safety standards. From their perspective, the markets clearly need more regulation and the WTO is the only body equipped with the power to provide stringent and effective food standards and to back them up with sanctions for countries that decide not to meet them.

Critics of the WTO and its growing power charge that the WTO already has too much control over setting food safety standards. They disparage the WTO's reliance on the Codex Alimentarius, a collection of internationally recognized standards and practices pertaining to foods, food production, and food safety established in 1963 by the Food and Agricultural Organization of the United States (FAO) and the World Health Organization (WHO). Managed and implemented by the Codex Alimentarius Commission, the Codex Alimentarius was created to protect the health of consumers and ensure fair practices in the international food trade. Critics charge, however, that the WTO utilizes the Codex more to maintain fair trade and advance its own political agenda than to protect the health of consumers.

The controversy over the WTO's role in creating and maintaining global food safety standards is one of the topics explored in the following chapter. Other viewpoints debate the WTO's role in facilitating global trade, improving human rights, and alleviating the global economic crisis.

> *"The WTO has . . . facilitated communication and transparency in the trading system."*

The WTO Facilitates Global Trade

Anne Effland, Mary Anne Normile, Donna Roberts, and John Wainio

Anne Effland, Mary Anne Normile, Donna Roberts, and John Wainio are contributors to Amber Waves, *a journal published by the U.S. Department of Agriculture's Economic Research Service. In the following viewpoint, they assert that the World Trade Organization has helped facilitate the growth of global trade. Focusing on agricultural trade policy, they describe how the WTO negotiates trade agreements and a way to enforce trade rules, which results in increased trade and economic gains for member countries.*

As you read, consider the following questions:

1. Why has the WTO become a focal point of the globalization controversy, according to the authors?

2. Since 1948, how has membership grown in the WTO, according to the authors?

Anne Effland, Mary Anne Normile, Donna Roberts, and John Wainio, "World Trade Organization and Globalization Help Facilitate Growth in Agricultural Trade," *Amber Waves*, June 2008. Reproduced by permission.

3. According to the authors, how many notifications from members documenting their policies for market access, domestic support, and export subsidies did the WTO's Committee on Agriculture review in 2006?

In simple terms, globalization refers to the closer integration of countries and people around the world. It is the product of numerous factors, including reduced trade barriers, lower transportation and communication costs, and increased movements of capital, knowledge, technology, culture, and people across borders. To many, these changes imply progress, but globalization is an issue of multiple dimensions that has sparked heated debates and protests around the world.

Proponents argue that globalization results in increased consumer choices and access, enables countries to use resources more efficiently, leads to the introduction of new technologies, creates new industries, and promotes more rapid economic growth.

WTO and Globalization

Critics maintain that globalization has exposed vulnerable economies to economic and financial shocks not of their making, contributed to environmental degradation, led to unemployment and downward pressure on wages, and strained the ability of poor countries to adapt.

In recent years, the World Trade Organization (WTO) has become a focal point of the globalization controversy, largely due to its visible role in reducing barriers to trade in goods and services. The massive protests at the 2001 WTO meeting in Seattle took many by surprise and thrust both globalization and the WTO into the world spotlight.

Critics of the WTO are not limited to anti-globalization protesters; proponents of free trade and globalization have also criticized the WTO. Some see the 7-year long negotiation of a new multilateral trade agreement as evidence that too many countries are unwilling to reach the compromises needed. Others cite the differences in expectations for developed and developing countries as a sign that the WTO is not even-handed. Still others see unacceptable threats to vulnerable industries and even to national sovereignty resulting from the disciplines required for membership.

Yet, since 1948, when the WTO's predecessor, the General Agreement on Tariffs and Trade (GATT), was launched, membership has grown from 23 to 151 countries. Another 30 countries hold observer status while they wait to become members. Given the criticism of the organization, why have so many countries joined?

Countries Seek Gains

Countries join the WTO for many reasons, but largely to increase trade, and, in particular, exports. One of the key contributions of economics has been its demonstration that countries can mutually benefit from trade. In its simplest form, if country A produces wheat and country B produces coffee, both can improve citizens' welfare by exchanging wheat for coffee. Through the price system, which establishes values for the exchange of multiple commodities, the process can be extended to accommodate an infinite variety of goods.

This simple yet powerful concept is behind much of the trend toward globalization and has motivated countries to negotiate trade agreements. Trade negotiations basically involve reciprocal concessions—exchanges of tariff cuts or other grants of comparable value that enable this mutually beneficial exchange of goods. A primary reason countries engage in trade negotiations is to increase access to foreign markets for their products. Granting access to foreign producers is seen as a necessary cost of gaining access to other markets. However, reducing trade barriers also can facilitate growth and benefit the overall economy by enabling a country to use its resources more efficiently.

The benefits of reciprocal trade concessions extend beyond the increased exports valued by producers: consumers also gain from concessions that lower the cost of imports. Trade policies, like tariffs, that raise the cost of imports essentially act as taxes on consumption. Lower tariffs and quotas, for example, have reduced the cost of many clothing items for U.S. consumers. Lower tariffs have also helped make a wider variety of fresh produce available to U.S. consumers during winter months. When economists measure the benefits of trade agreements, they include both the value of increased exports and the increase in well-being of consumers that comes from paying lower prices.

Economic Benefits of WTO Membership

Countries also seek membership in the WTO as a way to increase their potential for achieving economic growth and increased prosperity. For the generation of policy officials who witnessed the effects of protectionist policies on world economies during the Great Depression, the connection between trade and economic growth was clear. To remedy the policy mistakes of the 1930s and preceding decades, trade officials negotiated the 1947 GATT to lower barriers to international commerce and establish a charter setting out the broad principles that should govern trade policies.

Chief among these principles were the Most Favored Nation (MFN) and national treatment provisions. MFN mandated that importing countries would not be allowed to treat the same goods from the signatories of the GATT differently. National treatment mandated that imported goods should face the same regulatory standards as those imposed on the domestic goods of a member country. Both provisions convey powerful advantages to countries seeking access to foreign markets. Because of the MFN provision, a country joining the WTO today immediately qualifies for all the tariff concessions previously negotiated by members.

In the early years of GATT, membership meant participating in negotiations to reduce high tariffs that had restricted trade and led to economic hardship. Negotiations were conducted bilaterally and focused on the tariffs each country would like the other to reduce. Because the bilaterally negotiated concessions would be available to all GATT members through the MFN provision, other countries could balance those benefits against concessions they might be asked to make. For example, the U.S. could agree to cut a tariff on an import from another country even if it was not completely offset by an equivalent tariff cut by that country because the U.S. already expected to benefit from a tariff cut that country had negotiated with a third country.

As the membership in the GATT expanded, however, negotiators found it increasingly difficult and time consuming to complete bilateral deals. As a result, negotiations today follow a formula approach of across-the-board cuts. Deals among a large number of participants still offer countries the opportunity for balancing benefits against concessions.

WTO Facilitates Rule Enforcement

In addition to providing a forum for trade negotiations, multilateral trade agreements like GATT and the WTO extend a consistent set of rules to many countries at once. Countries agree to rules of trade that may limit their own policy flexibility because the rules impose discipline on the trade policies of other members—all countries accept some pain to realize gains.

The expectation that the rules of trade apply to all members of the multilateral agreement underlies reciprocal concessions. Each member is protected from rules violations by others. If one country raises a tariff above its agreed (or bound) ceiling level, for example, the injured country may be due compensation. This may come in the form of tariff reductions on other products or other trade concessions equal to the level of damage from the violation. The enforceable threat of retaliation embedded in reciprocal agreements creates a powerful incentive for members to comply with their obligations.

The original GATT system lacked a strong means of enforcing rules violations. Its dispute settlement process, which required consensus, allowed an importing country to unilaterally block trade complaints. Creation of the WTO provided the institutional framework to support a more effective dispute settlement process by providing measurable recourse to countries whose rights have been violated.

Adding to the original GATT rules, the WTO's Agreement on Agriculture and Agreement on the Application of Sanitary and Phytosanitary (SPS) Measures set out important provisions for governing trade in agricultural products. If issues related to a policy's compliance with trade rules cannot be resolved in bilateral discussions, countries can appeal to WTO committees that oversee the implementation of each individual agreement. For example, the Committee on Agriculture reviewed 155 notifications from members documenting their policies for market access, domestic support, and export subsidies in 2006. Likewise, the SPS Committee has provided a forum for airing grievances and made it easier to identify and track contentious regulations. The committee reports that one-third of the 245 "special trade concerns" identified by members over the past 12 years have been fully or partially resolved through consultations. The committee also has facilitated dispute resolutions between countries at every level of development.

WTO Resolves Trade Conflicts

Additional WTO dispute settlement mechanisms for resolving conflicts include adjudication by a WTO panel and the WTO Appellate Body, if required. If a disputed measure is found to violate WTO provisions, the parties to the dispute may request arbitration to determine a "reasonable period of time"

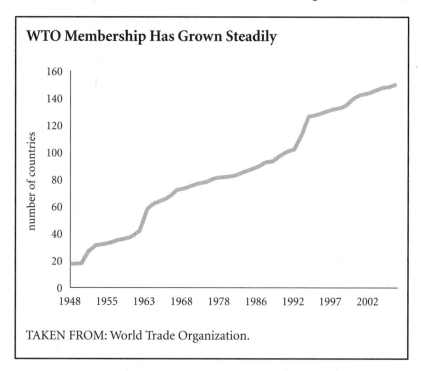

WTO Membership Has Grown Steadily

TAKEN FROM: World Trade Organization.

for the respondent to change its policy or, if it does not, to determine the amount of compensation or retaliation due to the complainant (usually in the form of tariff adjustments on other products).

The WTO has also facilitated communication and transparency in the trading system and helped to resolve disputes before they reach formal settlement proceedings. A strengthened requirement for transparency is among the important institutional changes brought about in the transition from GATT to WTO. Country "notifications," or reports to the WTO of proposed changes in policies or regulations that could adversely affect trade, are key to enabling judgment about the purpose, design, or effect of a policy or measure. WTO notification is now routine for all member countries. For example, members submitted more than 8,000 notifications related to SPS measures between 1995 and 2007, compared with fewer than 80 between 1980 and 1990.

The evidence indicates that these notifications spawned a broad-based "regulatory review," as major agricultural importers and exporters began to assess whether they and their trading partners were complying with the SPS Agreement. As a result, several measures restricting trade in fruit and vegetables were unilaterally revised following technical consultations. For example, Japan agreed to rescind its 46-year-old ban on several varieties of tomatoes grown in the United States based on scientific research indicating that the tomatoes were not afflicted with tobacco blue mold disease. New Zealand officially recognized that treating fruit with hot forced air was equivalent to spraying with a prohibited fumigant, thereby allowing several South Pacific countries to resume exports of mangos, papaya, and eggplant.

WTO Facilitates Globalization

Under GATT, and more recently through the WTO, member countries have reduced tariffs on manufactured goods to exceptionally low levels, facilitating a steady increase in trade in manufactured goods since the 1950s. Global trade in agricultural products, however, has grown much less rapidly since then for a number of reasons, including the continued protection of agriculture by many countries. The body of rules established to govern merchandise trade made numerous exceptions for agricultural goods. One of the most important accomplishments of the Uruguay Round [of trade talks] (1986–94) is that it succeeded in incorporating agriculture into the multilateral trade rules. Yet, agricultural trade continues to be influenced by a legacy of high protection and government intervention. Tariffs on agricultural products remain significantly higher, on average, than tariffs on manufactured goods.

Despite higher protection on agricultural trade, a number of factors have led to its growth over the past 40 years. Improvements in transportation and handling, such as containerization and refrigeration, have facilitated shipments of out-of-season produce from distant origins, something not possible 20 years earlier. Communication and logistical improvements have enabled shippers of bulk agricultural commodities, like grains, to respond more easily to market demands for specific types, grades, and qualities. Greater purchasing power among developing countries, which tend to spend a higher share of increased income on food, has also contributed to growth in agricultural trade. These developments have been complemented in recent years by the reductions in barriers to agricultural trade brought about through the Uruguay Round Agreement on Agriculture as well as through bilateral and regional agreements.

Globalization of agriculture can bring positive benefits for developing countries. Reduced global tariffs on processed products may fuel economic development by encouraging developing country exports of these products, allowing them to benefit from the employment and value-added benefits associated with domestic processing. Greater trade opportunities also may expand markets for their goods, making investment more attractive. Reducing subsidies also can help developing countries by encouraging shifts of resources to more efficient uses, in agriculture or other sectors.

Some WTO Countries Need Help

Successive rounds of multilateral trade liberalization, however, have revealed the difficulties that many low-income countries face in capturing the benefits of more open markets. In these countries, governments, institutions, and enterprises often lack capacities—in the form of information, policies, procedures, and infrastructure—to compete effectively in global markets and take full advantage of the opportunities that are offered through international trade. To help these countries overcome their trade-related institutional, human resource, and supply capacity constraints, WTO members have agreed on steps to improve implementation of the current agreements. These initiatives include increased technical and financial assistance in trade policy and regulations, trade development, and economic infrastructure.

Furthermore, in order to ease the adjustment pressures brought on by trade liberalization, developing countries are granted special and differential treatment within the WTO. In particular, developing countries are asked to make smaller cuts in tariffs than those for developed countries and are given a longer period of time to phase in the cuts. In addition, all countries have access to safeguard measures that allow them to temporarily restrain trade when their producers are threatened with serious injury as a result of imports.

Critics of the WTO have pointed to other limitations of the multilateral trading system, including the lack of agreements on environmental protection, labor standards, investment issues, and e-commerce. At the same time, the WTO has been attacked for tackling these other questions, which some consider peripheral to an agreement on trade. Attempts have been made to address some of these concerns in other forums, but these issues continue to be raised and are increasingly linked to globalization. The WTO may be further pressed to find a balance between what it views as its mandate to deal solely with trade rules and some of its members' views that through its trade rules, the WTO can make a contribution to addressing problems in other areas.

> "The WTO and its agreements are a powerful mechanism for spreading and locking in corporate-led globalization."

The WTO Advances Globalization and Harms Nations' Autonomy

Lori Wallach and Patrick Woodall

Lori Wallach is director of Public Citizen's Global Trade Watch division. Patrick Woodall is a senior policy analyst covering globalization of food and agriculture for Food and Water Watch. In the following viewpoint, they argue that the World Trade Organization's sprawling rules and regulations function to strong-arm nations into an existing global market designed by corporations and to undermine national autonomy by forcing nations to accept WTO rules and decisions in order to join.

As you read, consider the following questions:

1. How have WTO policies affected the number of people worldwide living on less than $1 a day, according to the authors?

2. What did Wallach and Woodall report that a UNCTAD study said about the relationship between developing countries and rapid trade liberalization?

3. According to the authors, how are corporations manipulating countries to change the trade policies in other countries?

M any people are surprised when they first learn that trade is only a small element of the WTO.

But the World Trade Organization—and the sprawling rules that it enforces—actually covers a huge array of subjects not included in past trade agreements that extend far beyond trade matters. The new agreements that were established with the WTO nine years ago [in 1995] included 800-plus pages of one-size-fits-all rules. Those new agreements set constraints on signatory countries' *domestic food* safety standards, environmental and product safety rules, service-sector regulation, investment and development policy, intellectual property standards, government procurement rules, and more.

WTO and Trade

The establishment of the WTO transformed the nature of global "trade" agreements. The General Agreement on Tariffs and Trade (GATT), a 1947 pact that had governed tariffs and quotas on trade in goods, had included some simple—and objective—principles, like requiring countries to apply the same regulations to foreign and domestic goods. But the new WTO rules are subjective—constraining the *level* of food safety or environmental protection a country can provide or the priorities a country can choose—even if these policies treat domestic and foreign goods equally. Some of the new WTO agreements also force countries to implement specific policies in their domestic laws. For instance, all countries are required to implement certain intellectual property rules, including giving patent owners decades of monopoly control over a vast array of items including plant varieties, seeds, and other things we do not ordinarily think of as private property. Instead of setting terms for *inter*national trade—exchange between different nations—these rules are aimed at eliminating the diversity of national policies, priorities, and cultures to create the uniform world market sought by large multinational corporations.

A key WTO provision specifically requires each signatory to ensure the conformity of its laws, regulations and administrative procedures to the WTO agreements' terms. WTO member nations can challenge as an "illegal trade barrier" any national or local policy of another WTO country, bringing charges before a WTO tribunal comprised of three trade officials who meet behind closed doors. Nations whose policies are judged not to conform with WTO rules are ordered to eliminate them or face permanent trade sanctions.

WTO and Globalization

Taken as a whole, the WTO and its agreements are a powerful mechanism for spreading and locking in corporate-led globalization. The WTO is a mechanism to bring every country in the world—ready or not—into an existing global market designed by corporations, and to take the practices those corporations invented willy-nilly—which, of course, suit their needs—and set them in stone as "WTO rules."

Because its terms are so broad, the WTO has managed to intervene in domestic policies all over the planet. India, like many countries, once had a ban on the patenting of seeds and medicines, to make them broadly accessible. A WTO challenge claiming India had failed to implement the required twenty-year patenting system resulted in India reversing its ban—threatening to deprive millions of people of life-giving resources. In Guatemala, implementation of the UNICEF–World Health Organization Code on the labeling of infant formula was gutted after a WTO threat. Consumers and producers in Europe face costly trade sanctions because the European Union

(EU) has not implemented a WTO order to import beef containing artificial hormones—the WTO ruled that Europe's standards provided too much consumer protection after a U.S. WTO attack. Meanwhile, a U.S. WTO case forced the EU to eliminate a program that had set aside a small market share for bananas from former Caribbean colonies, leading to the ruin of thousands of small family farms in several island nations. Policies aimed at ensuring the continued existence of some Canadian news magazines in the face of massive U.S. magazine imports were abolished after a successful U.S. WTO case. On the other hand, the U.S. saw its gasoline cleanliness standards weakened after a WTO assault on Clean Air Act regulations by several countries. Even though the U.S. signed a global environmental treaty called the Convention on International Trade in Endangered Species, American rules requiring shrimp fishers not to kill sea turtles were diluted after a WTO challenge to U.S. Endangered Species Act regulations enforcing the treaty. Meanwhile, the U.S. State Department, lobbying about how a state law might violate WTO, pressured Maryland legislators to drop a procurement policy aimed at promoting human rights in Nigeria. These are only a few of the negative results of nine years of WTO implementation.

Little to Do with Trade

Proponents of this system have called it "free trade" and attack all who criticize it as "protectionist" or "isolationist"—a great irony given the international nature of the opposition. Yet, the WTO's rules have little to do with trade and even less to do with the nineteenth-century free trade philosophies of [economics patriarchs] Adam Smith or David Ricardo.

Indeed, some of the topics covered by the WTO have so little to do with trade that naming these agreements required explanation. Thus, WTO includes an Agreement on Trade Related Intellectual Property and an Agreement on Trade Related Investment. One longtime WTO observer often quips that you can identify which WTO agreements have the least connection to trade by which have the "Trade Related" label slapped on them.

If such an autocratic, antidemocratic system had been imposed on elected governments around the world by force, human rights monitors and UN inspectors would have been dispatched. Instead, the WTO's silent coup d'état will only be reversed by citizen activism and campaigning. A first step for many people is realizing that "trade" is the least of what is covered by the WTO's rules, and then realizing what that means for their daily lives. . . .

Gains Fail to Materialize

We must await full implementation of the Uruguay Round Agreements before we can fully assess their long-term economic impacts. But the economic trends that have emerged so far indicate serious problems. These trends would have to abruptly reverse course to merely return the developing world to better, pre–Uruguay Round conditions, much less to fulfill many of the outlandish predictions of broad benefits served up by Uruguay Round boosters. Unbelievably, WTO boosters still argue that the answer to this grinding poverty is more of the same, faster—including a new proposed WTO expansion—and that poverty is being caused by governments not adhering quickly or completely enough to the WTO formula.

Thankfully, the ironclad consensus among economists and policy elites around the world in favor of the model promoted by the WTO rules has loosened dramatically. For some, theory and ideology have been overcome by the facts: the number of people living on less than $1 a day (the World Bank's definition of extreme poverty) has risen since the WTO went into effect and, in many parts of the world, the percentage of people living is such that extreme poverty also has risen. What we also know today and what has contributed greatly to the shift among elites is that the world has been buffeted by unprecedented financial instability as more countries have adopted the package of policies in the WTO. Economic growth in the developing world has slowed. Income inequality is rising rapidly between and within countries. A report by the United Nations Conference on Trade and Development (UNCTAD) found that, "In almost all developing countries that have undertaken rapid trade liberalization, wage inequality has increased, most often in the context of declining industrial employment of unskilled workers and large absolute falls in their real wages, on the order of 20–30% in Latin American countries."

Despite productivity gains, wages in many countries have failed to rise. Commodity prices are at all-time lows, causing the standard of living for many people to slide, particularly in Asia, Latin America, and Africa. Indeed, in most countries the period under the Uruguay Round has brought dramatic reversals in fortune—and not for the better.

Reversals of Fortune

Latin America is foundering, mired in its deepest economic slump since the debt crisis of the 1980s. The corporate economic globalization model with its hallmark of "free" trade, export-oriented development, privatization, and investment liberalization was imposed on Argentina by multilateral institutions such as the IMF [International Monetary Fund], the World Bank, and the WTO. Argentina reorganized its entire political and economic structure to comply with this model, and it was highlighted as a "poster child" for the new global economy—until it imploded with desperate and violent consequences.

East Asia lost decades of economic progress in a crisis caused in part by the very investment and financial service-sector deregulation that WTO rules intensify and spread to other nations. When the U.S. media announced that the crisis was over in 1999, people living in Asia knew better. For instance, in Korea the crisis had quadrupled unemployment and precipitated a 200% increase in absolute poverty.

Global economic indicators generally paint a tragic picture: The median income of the tenth of the world's people living in the richest countries was 77 times greater than the tenth in the poorest in 1980, but by 1999, the richest earned 122 times the poorest countries. Entire regions of the developing world are falling alarmingly behind the wealthiest countries that compose the Organization for Economic Cooperation and Development (OECD). Sub-Saharan Africa's per capita income was one sixth of OECD countries in 1975, but fell to one fourteenth of OECD per capita income in 2000. Over the same period, Latin America and the Caribbean per capita income fell from less than half that of OECD countries to less than a third, and Arab countries' per capita income fell from one quarter of that of OECD countries to one fifth.

U.S. Economic Indicators

In the U.S., the trade deficit is at an all-time high, $435 billion in 2002 and climbing, having ballooned—not declined as promised—from $98 billion before WTO in 1994. The median family income has not risen by $1,700 per year during *any* of the past nine years as promised, despite the fact that the U.S. had a period of unprecedented economic growth. Since the WTO went into effect, the U.S. has seen its industrial base hollowed out with the loss of 2 million manufacturing jobs. Now the service sector and high-tech jobs that we were told by the WTO's supporters would be our employment future are beginning to follow the manufacturing jobs to low-wage countries, with more than 3 million U.S. jobs expected to be shifted to China and other nations by 2015, according to Forrester Research. Meanwhile, analysis of promised future gains of greater trade liberalization shows that net losses—not gains—would result for most people from further liberalization.

An Economist on Globalization

Economist Jagdish Bhagwati of Columbia University has been one of the most visible and resolute intellectual advocates for free-market globalization, but lately he sounds a lot like Lori Wallach, the brainy lawyer who leads Global Trade Watch. "The process of trade liberalization is becoming a sham," Bhagwati wrote recently in the *Financial Times*, "the ultimate objective being the capture, reshaping and distortion of the WTO in the image of American lobbying interests."

Wallach and other leaders of worldwide popular dissent have been making the same argument about bait-and-switch diplomacy for a decade. "Oh, absolutely," Bhagwati exclaims. "People like Lori Wallach are right." The multinational corporate interests essentially hijacked the pure "free trade" principles Bhagwati espouses and turned "free-trade agreements" into their own agenda for a densely layered legal code—investment rules that impose a straitjacket of do's and don'ts on developing-country governments.

William Greider, Nation, *September 4, 2003.*

While the economic data demonstrate the absolute failure of the WTO model, they are but one part of the story. Of equal importance, but less well known, is the WTO's consistent record of eroding public-interest policies designed to safeguard the environment, our families' health and safety, human rights, and democracy.

Undermining Public Interest

Since it was created in 1995, the WTO has ruled that every environmental, health or safety policy it has reviewed but one is an illegal trade barrier that must be eliminated or changed. With few exceptions, nations whose laws were declared trade barriers by the WTO—or that were merely threatened with prospective WTO action—have eliminated or watered down their policies to meet WTO requirements. In addition to undermining existing public-interest safeguards, this trend has a chilling effect on countries' inclinations to pass new environmental, human rights, or safety laws.

The WTO's tribunals systematically rule against domestic laws challenged as violating WTO rules. As of January 2003, defending countries have won just 13 out of 88 completed WTO cases—or only 14.8%. (The United States lost two of those three anomalous cases.) Developing countries are among the biggest losers in this system. They generally do not have the money and expertise to either bring cases to the WTO or defend themselves before the WTO. Many simply amend their laws as soon as a WTO threat is issued. As a result, the WTO's full damage to domestic policy is much greater than the WTO's official case record shows. With few exceptions, no one knows about those instances when domestic policies are changed before formal WTO cases are initiated. . . .

Real-Life Examples of WTO Rules

Consider what happened to the United States' attempt to reduce emissions from automobiles. The U.S. relaxed its standards designed to limit gasoline contaminants after Venezuela won a WTO challenge against Clean Air Act regulations that it claimed unfairly affected its gasoline industry. In a classic example of WTO double-talk, the panel in this case ruled that a country was free to choose any environmental policy it desired, but could only implement policies that were consistent with WTO rules. The [Bill] Clinton administration implemented new regulations that it had previously rejected as being effectively unenforceable in order to comply with the WTO order.

Further, WTO rules prohibit countries from treating physically similar products differently based on how they are made or harvested, putting in limbo many laws, like those banning drift-net fishing or requiring less polluting manufacturing processes; as well as laws banning goods made with child labor. For instance, in the eyes of the WTO, tuna caught in dolphin-safe nets should be treated no differently than tuna caught in nets that ensnare dolphins. After Mexico threatened to go to the WTO to enforce a GATT ruling against a U.S. law designed to prevent dolphins from being killed in tuna nets, the Clinton administration worked with some of Congress's leading anti-environmental members to water down the popular U.S. policy. Now, after renewed threats of WTO action, the Bush administration is trying to change the definition of "dolphin safe" on tuna can labels to allow its use on tuna caught with deadly encirclement nets. Only an emergency injunction issued in an ongoing court case has temporarily halted the new policy.

WTO rules launch a race to the bottom by setting a ceiling but no floor on environmental protection and public health and safety. Domestic standards on health, the environment and public safety that are higher than international ones must pass a set of stringent tests in order not to be considered trade barriers. There is no requirement that international standards be met, only that they cannot be exceeded.

Human Health and Safety

A WTO ruling against Europe's ban on beef grown using artificial hormones is a vivid and alarming illustration of the WTO's unacceptable approach to human health and safety. The WTO declared that Europe's ban on meat tainted with artificial growth hormones had to go because the WTO-recognized food standards—from a corporate-influenced body called the Codex Alimentarius—considered such artificial hormones safe. The WTO also said that the ban was WTO-illegal because the Europeans had not scientifically demonstrated that the artificial hormone residues in meat pose an explicit threat to human health, although it is known that the hormones themselves do. The EU refused to cave in to U.S. pressure to accept the beef its consumers do not want. As a result it was hit with $116.8 million per year in WTO-authorized trade sanctions which remain in place.

The WTO system effectively turns the very premise by which most progressive governments have handled food safety and other human health-related policies on its head. Generally, manufacturers are required to prove that a product is safe before it can be sold, and countries ban the product until the company has submitted the proof. Under WTO rules, governments must prove that a product is unsafe before they can ban it.

Corporations Use the WTO

Another alarming aspect of the WTO system is how nations are effectively used by corporations to challenge policies in other countries. The U.S. was going to bat for Chiquita, the banana giant, when it successfully attacked Europe's preferential treatment of bananas from former EU colonies in the WTO case mentioned above. The U.S. does not produce bananas for export, and most of Chiquita's employees are underpaid farm workers laboring on its vast Central American plantations. The EU rescinded its preferential treatment, devastating many small, independent Caribbean banana farmers. The ultimate result could be destabilization of the very economic foundations of the Caribbean's numerous small democratic nations, meaning U.S. national interest in the region—in drug interdiction, political stability, trade and tourism—could be undermined by the WTO action taken on behalf of Chiquita.

But a country need not always actually challenge another country's laws to change them. Often, the mere threat of a challenge suffices. Most of these cases remain undocumented. However, one known example is the U.S. threat against Guatemala's implementation of the so-called Nestle's Code. Decades of promotion by infant formula corporations resulted in a plague of needless infant deaths that occurred when mothers in developing countries mixed formula with unsanitary water. Reacting to this public health crisis and a global campaign, UNICEF and the World Health Organization created a global code on infant formula marketing which one hundred-plus countries implemented. Sometimes known as the "Nestle's Code," it banned infant formula packaging that depicted healthy, fat babies to ensure that women, particularly illiterate ones, wouldn't associate baby formula with healthy infants and be discouraged from breast-feeding. Gerber Foods, the company whose trademarked logo includes a pudgy, happy infant, took exception to Guatemala's implementation of the Code.

The Gerber Case

When Guatemala insisted that Gerber remove the baby image from the packaging of products distributed in Guatemala, the company refused, arguing that under the WTO's intellectual property rules, its trademark baby face trumped the health treaty. The U.S. State Department sent a letter to the president of Guatemala threatening a trade case. Defending a case at the WTO can cost hundreds of thousands of dollars. In Guatemala's case, it was a choice between using that money for other public health initiatives, or gambling it on an uncertain outcome before a WTO tribunal. The government decided to weaken the law—by exempting imported breast-milk substitutes—rather than risk the expense for what might be a losing defense. Prior to this, Guatemala had been promoted by UNICEF as a country whose successful implementation of the Code had cut infant mortality.

And while many Americans saw news coverage of Vice President Al Gore's campaign events being protested by AIDS activists, few realized that a WTO threat was underlying this brouhaha. South Africa's efforts to make AIDS treatment more accessible to its population was attacked by international pharmaceutical companies and the Clinton administration as violating patent rights required by the WTO. Global campaigning and pressure ultimately forced a declaration to be issued at the 2001 WTO Doha Ministerial recognizing that the WTO rules in fact do not bar practices such as compulsory licensing for generic production of medicine. However, prior to that, the U.S. filed a formal WTO challenge against Brazilian pharmaceutical policy. Brazil is recognized worldwide as having the most effective public health approach to HIV/AIDS, and its policy of making antiretroviral drugs available to every infected citizen has saved the lives of millions.

The U.S. ultimately withdrew its WTO challenge against Brazil as public pressure on the issue grew. However, in recent WTO talks, the [George W.] Bush administration singlehandedly blocked a WTO agreement which would have clarified that WTO rules allow poor nations to import affordable drugs that have been produced in other countries under compulsory licenses—a practice necessary for the many nations without manufacturing capacity.

Beyond these cases, which are sufficiently disturbing in themselves, lies an unnerving theme: In the WTO forum, global commerce takes precedence over everything—democracy, public health, equity, access to essential services, the environment, food safety and more.

| "A successful outcome of the [WTO's] Doha Development Round can be part of the solution to the economic downturn."

The WTO Can Help Solve the Global Economic Crisis

Pascal Lamy

Pascal Lamy is the director-general of the World Trade Organization. In the following speech to the International Chamber of Commerce (ICC), he acknowledges that the global economic crisis has spurred fears and pessimism across the globe, which in turn has political leaders turning away from global free trade policies. Instead, Lamy argues, trade should be considered part of the solution to the economic crisis, not part of the problem.

As you read, consider the following questions:

1. What does Lamy describe as the mood of the 2009 Davos Conference among political, business, and union leaders?

2. What are the world growth projections in 2009, according to the author?

Pascal Lamy, "Trade Is Part of the Solution to the Global Economic Crisis," World Trade Organization, February 3, 2009. Reproduced by permission.

3. What does Lamy say caused the severe financial crisis present in 2009?

In 1919, a handful of entrepreneurs decided to create an organization that would represent business everywhere. They were determined to bring hope to a world still devastated by the First World War, which had just ended. They resolved to replace fear and suspicion with a new spirit of friendly international cooperation among business people. They founded the International Chamber of Commerce [ICC] and called themselves "the merchants of peace".

In the 1920s the ICC focused on reparations and war debts. At that time the world had few working international structures and no world system of rules to govern trade relations. A decade later, it struggled through the years of depression to hold back the tide of protectionism and economic nationalism. The ICC saw the creation of the multilateral trading system with the birth of the GATT [General Agreement on Tariffs and Trade], the predecessor of the WTO, and contributed to its strengthening to the current day.

And today [in 2009], as we celebrate the International Chamber's 90th anniversary, the ICC has again demonstrated its commitment to a more open multilateral trading system with the launch of the ICC Research Foundation. I would like to compliment Victor Fung and Marcus Wallenberg for taking this initiative that will undoubtedly contribute to a better understanding of the benefits of a more open and regulated multilateral trading system. Stimulating intellectual leadership and a broader understanding of what works best in support of the public interest will certainly add to a more balanced and considered debate on the benefits of trade opening.

Poor Economy Spurs Fear

This is all the more important, given the state of the world economy today. Like many of you, I have just returned from the annual World Economic Forum meeting in Davos [Switzerland]. Much of what I heard there from political, business and union leaders can be summarized by the words "pessimism" and "fear".

Fear of massive job losses. Fear of lack of credit even for relatively safe operations, such as those to finance trade transactions. Fear of a sharp decrease in trade which is stalling an important engine for growth, especially for many developing countries.

The world growth projections today are at 0 per cent, with developed countries posting a negative growth of -2 per cent and developing countries a positive one of around 5 per cent. The positive growth comes from emerging countries which are highly dependent on trade. With the forecast that global export volumes will contract by -2 per cent in 2009, many emerging economies have sounded the alarm bell.

Trade has become another casualty of the recession provoked by the severe financial crisis caused by lack of regulation, supervision and excess. In these times of serious economic crisis, our biggest challenge today is to ensure trade is part of the solution and not part of the problem.

Isolationism Is the Enemy

In this period of uncertainty and fear, calls for a stronger role for governments and regulators to intervene resonate well. But for this to be successful, all actors have to agree on common targets and enemies, and work together. Global cooperation within and across countries is therefore of the essence. At times of global economic crisis, enemy number one is isolationism.

We still remember the 1930 Smoot and Hawley Act sharply raising US tariffs on more than 20,000 products. We also remember that many other countries retaliated, raising their tariffs on US goods. The Great Depression followed. Whether it is with tariffs or with new, more sophisticated faces of Smoot

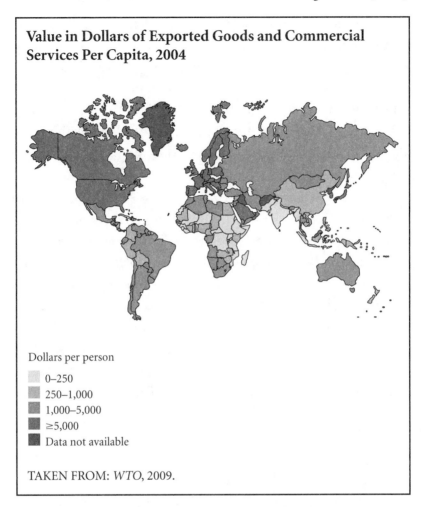

Value in Dollars of Exported Goods and Commercial Services Per Capita, 2004

Dollars per person

- 0–250
- 250–1,000
- 1,000–5,000
- ≥5,000
- Data not available

TAKEN FROM: *WTO*, 2009.

and Hawley, today we run the risk of sliding down a slippery slope of tit-for-tat measures. It was Mahatma Gandhi who said "an eye for an eye makes the whole world blind".

Ladies and gentlemen, paraphrasing Gandhi today we could say that "if it is a job for a job, then we will have massive unemployment".

What the WTO Is Doing

To help WTO members have a better and real-time idea of global trends in international trade and trade policy developments, we have set up a radar tracking trade and trade-related measures taken in the context of the current crisis. [In early February 2009] the radar picture showed that most WTO members appear to have successfully kept domestic protectionist pressures under control. In the meantime, a new spot has appeared with the "Buy America" provision in the draft US stimulus package to be considered by the US Senate.

Protection, yes; isolationism, no. Governments must provide answers to the social unrest which is brewing behind the massive job losses. This is the time to activate social safety nets, not only in rich countries because there are also poor in rich societies. But also, and in particular, in the poorer countries who do not have the means to weather the storm. The stimulus packages that have been adopted need to provide answers to those who are being left behind in this crisis.

And it is in this context that we all risk seeing trade and the WTO lumped together with the elements of the Washington consensus which many believe to have failed. With deregulation and privatisations. And it is now that we risk throwing the baby out with the bath water.

Trade Integral to Economic Recovery

This is why now more than ever it is time to stress the value of trade as a multiplier of growth and the value of the multilateral trading system, with its 60 years of global regulation, as an insurance policy against protectionism. I would humbly ask that these issues be included on the to-do list for the ICC Research Foundation that we are launching today.

This is the time to invest in the WTO and strengthen the global rules-based system which has so carefully been constructed over the last 60 years. A conclusion of the Doha Development Round of negotiations is therefore all the more relevant and urgent.

Many of the trade ministers who I met in Davos last week mentioned that trade is an integral part of the stimulus packages that are being adopted. In my view it is in fact an essential part of the recovery package.

Doha Negotiations Are Vital

Let's be frank: this crisis will take much more than a Doha deal to restore the path of growth. But a successful outcome of the Doha Development Round can be part of the solution to the economic downturn. It will also send the political signal that at harsh and difficult times, governments are capable of working together to provide the kind of global answer which is so desperately needed.

This is why WTO members should pick up from where they left off in 2008 and enter the negotiating arena with renewed commitment. I am encouraged to find support in this respect from many political leaders around the world and I count on them to show the way forward.

We have accomplished around 80 per cent of our set targets in the Doha Round. But with the necessary political guidance, the willingness to compromise and realistic expectations, I am convinced that we can conclude these negotiations rapidly.

ICC Involvement Essential

It goes without saying that this cannot be done without the support and active involvement of the business community. The ICC has been exemplary in this respect and I count on you and your members to continue to be supporters of more open trade and stronger multilateral rules. I realize full well that these are very tough times for the business community, but I urge all of you to show restraint when the crisis bites and to continue to champion the ICC's core mission.

Let me end by wishing the ICC success in the newly established Research Foundation. I am convinced that in 10 years from now, when the ICC celebrates its 100th anniversary and the WTO has only vague memories of the once so difficult Doha Round, history will prove us right. That our conviction and dedication to a more open and equitable world trading system is our contribution to a more peaceful and prosperous planet.

> *"The WTO's Financial Services Agreement (FSA) locked in domestically, and exported internationally, the model of extreme financial service deregulation that most analysts consider a prime cause of the current crisis."*

The WTO Helped Cause the Global Economic Crisis

Public Citizen

Public Citizen is a national nonprofit organization established in 1971 to lobby on behalf of consumer interests, with a focus on economic justice. In the following viewpoint from one of its policy primers, the author traces the connection between the World Trade Organization's expansive financial services deregulation requirements and the global financial and economic meltdown that hit in 2008. Public Citizen argues that the connection is causal and that only significant reforms to the WTO's General Agreement on Trade in Services (GATS) will allow countries to recover from and address the root causes of the worldwide financial crisis.

Public Citizen, "The Connection Between the World Trade Organization's Extreme Financial Service Deregulation Requirements and the Global Economic Crisis," December 2008. Reproduced by permission.

As you read, consider the following questions:

1. How does the WTO Secretariat describe the implications of the GATS rules, according to Public Citizen?

2. According to the author, how many countries signed on to the Financial Services Agreement in 1999?

3. According to Public Citizen, how is the United States affected by WTO financial rules?

Amidst breathless calls from all quarters for expansive new global financial services regulations addressing the global economic crisis is a seemingly total lack of awareness that most of the world's countries are bound to expansive World Trade Organization (WTO) financial services deregulation requirements. The WTO's Financial Services Agreement (FSA) locked in domestically, and exported internationally, the model of extreme financial service deregulation that most analysts consider a prime cause of the current crisis. Deregulation (not only liberalization) of the financial service sector—including banking, insurance, asset management, pension funds, securities, and more—is among the most important, but least discussed, aspects of the WTO.

Yet, to date, the only connections most policymakers are drawing between the WTO and the current crisis are of the red-herring variety: panicky warnings about countries increasing tariffs to block imports in response to dire economic conditions. Consider the communiqué issued from the November 15 [2008] Washington G-20 Summit, a meeting ostensibly convened so that countries could agree to new domestic and international financial sector regulations needed to respond to the crisis. The declaration called for the completion of WTO Doha Round negotiations, which includes as one of its three central pillars further financial service sector deregulation. The communiqué also called for countries to "refrain from raising new barriers to investment or to trade in goods and services . . . or implementing WTO inconsistent measures" for 12 months.

How to Address the Meltdown

Yet, in recent months, the [George W.] Bush administration and governments worldwide have taken various measures to counter the crisis that contradict the fundamental precepts of the current globalization model—and indeed in some cases violate the rules implementing this model, such as those of the WTO. Many of the most basic national and international remedies now being proposed to fix the mess and avoid future meltdowns occupy policy space that governments have ceded to the WTO.

Remedying the crisis will require significant changes to the WTO's General Agreement on Trade in Services (GATS), and specifically its 1997 Financial Services Agreement and numerous countries' commitments under these pacts. Further, unless the [Barack] Obama administration takes speedy action to remove the outrageous new, additional deregulation commitments now on the Doha Round negotiating table, this Bush trade-policy hangover will undermine attempts to remedy the financial crisis here and abroad.

WTO Forces Deregulation

Many people still assume our trade pacts are about traditional matters, such as tariff cuts; in fact, today's "trade" pacts like the WTO require signatory countries—including the United States—to conform their domestic policies to an expansive *non-trade* deregulatory agenda. One of the most controversial WTO agreements is GATS, which sets out rules for how countries can regulate the "service sectors" of their economies. The WTO Secretariat was unusually direct in describing the implications of the GATS rules: *"Governments are free in principle to pursue any national policy objectives provided the relevant measures are compatible with the GATS."*

One of the most controversial service sectors covered by the GATS is the financial sector. When many countries initially rejected the extreme banking and insurance deregulation agenda being pushed by U.S. and European governments and corporations, special additional negotiations were launched after the WTO was established. Thus, the WTO's limits on domestic financial service regulation are contained not only in the original GATS, but in the subsequent Financial Services Agreement, which went into effect in 1999 with 105 countries signed on, as well as the Understanding on Commitments in Financial Services, to which the OECD [Organization for Economic Cooperation and Development] countries also signed. Domestic policies which do not conform with the extensive regulatory limits in these agreements are subject to challenge in the WTO's powerful despite resolution system. Policies that are judged by WTO tribunals to violate the rules must be eliminated or trade sanctions can be imposed on the non-conforming country until the policy is changed.

In the case of the United States, WTO commitments to stay out of regulation of "banking," "other financial services" and "insurance" are extremely broad. The United States signed on to extra WTO obligations agreed to by OECD countries that include a "standstill" commitment—meaning we are forbidden from rolling back deregulation (or liberalization) of the expansive financial services we bound to comply with WTO rules. Translated out of GATS-ese, this means that the United States has bound itself not to do what Congress, regulators and scholars deem necessary—create new financial service regulations. This agreement also includes a commitment for signatories to eliminate domestic financial service regulatory policies that *meet* GATS rules, but that may still "*adversely affect the ability of financial service suppliers of any other (WTO) Member to operate, compete, or enter*" the market. The United States is also bound to ensure that foreign financial service suppliers are permitted "to offer in its territory any

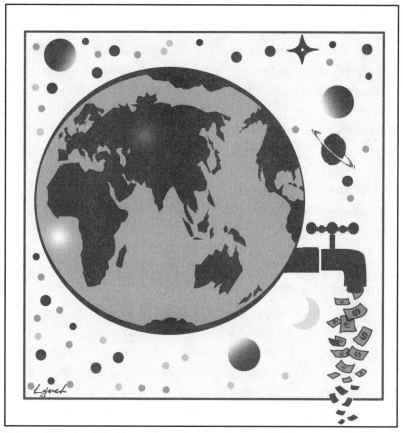

"Money down the drain," by Mark Lynch. www.cartoonstock.com.

new financial service," a direct conflict with the various proposals to limit various risky investment instruments.

The Glass-Steagall Act

Meanwhile, the list of reasonable financial service regulations that actually do *not* meet even the core GATS requirements is lengthy, demonstrating why altering this agreement is a necessary aspect of remedying the current crisis. For instance, consider the use of "firewalls" between various financial services so that trouble in one sector does not contaminate the entire system. The Glass-Steagall Act of 1933, which forbade bank holding companies from operating other financial services, applied such firewalls so as to avoid a repeat of the financial collapse that occurred during the Great Depression. While the law applied to domestic and foreign banks alike, it had the effect of preventing foreign banks that combined commercial and investment banking services from entering the U.S. market. But various U.S. GATS "market-access" commitments in banking services guarantee such access. The [Bill] Clinton administration, which conducted WTO Financial Service agreement negotiations, recognized this conflict and indeed made a commitment explicitly listed in the U.S. GATS schedule to "fix" this problem. The provisions of Glass-Steagall that prohibited a bank holding company from owning other financial companies were repealed with passage of the Gramm-Leach-Bliley Act in 1999, the year the WTO Financial Service Agreement went into effect.

Sorting out exactly what modicum of policy space remains under these rules requires reviewing the more than 30 pages of financial service sector commitments made by the United States. However, consider just one sector that has been a focus of considerable attention as a source of the financial meltdown: "Trading of Securities and Derivative Products and Services Related Thereto." The only carve-out that the United States listed regarding regulation of derivatives is for *onion futures*—seriously.

The Damage Wrought by the WTO

Few in Congress even reviewed the thousands of pages comprising the Uruguay Agreements Act in 1994 which implemented the WTO. With this Fast Tracked vote, Congress bound nearly 100 sectors of the U.S. service economy to GATS constraints with little understanding or discussion. The 1997 WTO FSA, which imposed drastic new limits on Congress' regulatory authority over financial service, was never even sent to Congress. Meanwhile, creating worldwide limits on domestic regulation of financial services via the WTO was the project of the large financial service firms that Congress was supposed to be regulating for the public interest. [According to a Brookings Institution report,] "An important distinguishing feature of the FSA relates to the degree of support and the political legitimacy it generated through a shared sense of transatlantic purpose and commitment on the part of the financial services industry itself. The sector was truly unique in that respect, and there is little doubt within the trade policy community that financial sector support in the European Union and the United States was a determining force in concluding the FSA."

Over the past century, U.S. financial regulation has shifted from strict financial controls over banking and capital markets following the Great Depression to deregulation in the 1980s and 1990s. The WTO locks in the U.S. status quo at a time of unprecedented financial liberalization and foreseeable damage wrought by this model to the U.S. and global economy.

Altering the WTO financial services rules is critical for creating domestic policy space to address the crisis. The United States—and U.S.-based financial service firms—used WTO negotiations to export the U.S. model of extreme financial service deregulation to 105 other WTO signatory countries who are bound under the Financial Service Agreement. For these countries to establish new financial service regulations—and to further the goal of new global regulations—the existing WTO limits must be eliminated. However, even in the face of this crisis, the push for further financial services liberalization continues at WTO. On the table now in the WTO Doha Round negotiations are proposals for *further* financial services deregulation—tabled by the United States, the European Union and other countries that have been busy ignoring *existing* WTO terms because doing so is the necessary to counter the crisis.

| "WTO rules are giving individuals and firms new rights."

The WTO Can Promote Human Rights

Susan Ariel Aaronson and Jamie M. Zimmerman

Susan Ariel Aaronson and Jamie M. Zimmerman are the codirectors of the Human Rights and Trade Partnership Project at the Kenan Institute at the University of North Carolina. In the following viewpoint, they contend that the World Trade Organization can appease its many critics by implementing measures that include improving human rights along with increasing global trade. In fact, Aaronson and Zimmerman argue, significant progress has been made in China, where meeting WTO requirements resulted in more freedoms and opportunity for redress and dispute settlement.

As you read, consider the following questions:

1. What are member countries forced to do to meet WTO obligations, according to the authors?

2. According to Aaronson and Zimmerman, how can the WTO trade settlement system empower citizens?

3. What more do the authors believe that the WTO can do to advance human rights?

Representatives from some 150 governments, civil society groups, and businesses will probably not have an altogether pleasant experience at this week's [in December 2005] Hong Kong Ministerial. Trade negotiators may not hear the shouts of thousands of protestors in their air conditioned conference venues, but the world will see them and hear their complaints. Many of these protestors will argue that the WTO enhances the power of multinational corporations and industrialized country governments at the expense of the world's poor. This perspective will resonate in many quarters.

Yet neither supporters nor critics of the WTO see the full picture of the trade body's role in the global economy. As WTO detractors argue, the WTO should do more to examine its impact on internationally accepted human rights. Yet these same critics should acknowledge an interesting side effect of WTO membership. Without deliberate intent, the WTO is altering the balance of power between member governments and their citizens.

WTO Can Make a Difference

In order to meet WTO obligations, member countries must provide specific economic and procedural rights for their citizens. These rights include property rights, legal guarantees, the right to submit comments about specific trade policies to a national agency, and the right to appeal administrative rulings on trade. Moreover, WTO members must establish these rights in domestic law and ensure they are enforced. Many new members of the WTO have had to develop new laws, regulations, and enforcement expertise to meet these obligations. Moreover, they must apply the same rules and regulations to domestic and foreign market actors. If these governments do not take these steps, their trade policies can be challenged through the WTO system of binding dispute settlement.

WTO rules are giving individuals and firms new rights. The WTO requires its members to devise transparent means of protecting and enforcing certain economic rights such as intellectual property rights. When China joined the WTO, it was obligated to establish new laws that accord both its citizens and foreign producers exclusive intellectual property rights (IPR) to copyrights, trade marks, patents, industrial designs, etc. . . . Chinese policymakers now understand that they must protect these rights in order to encourage innovation. Despite that recognition, China has done a poor job of protecting these IPR. In the past, domestic and foreign intellectual property holders could do little more than complain to Chinese authorities. But now both Chinese and foreign intellectual property owners can benefit from the WTO's dispute settlement system. [In December 2005] the United States, Japanese, and Swiss governments filed a formal request with the WTO for information from China on the country's IPR enforcement efforts. Based on these findings, the US and its allies may challenge Chinese enforcement of IPR under binding WTO dispute settlement mechanisms. If they are successful in that dispute, China would have to change its ways or risk retaliation as well as lower levels of foreign investment.

WTO Dispute Settlement

That same binding system of dispute settlement provides another example of how WTO rules can empower citizens with new rights under international law. Developing and middle income countries are using trade disputes to challenge subsidies that undermine the ability of small farmers in the developing world to sell their goods at home and abroad. For example, the Brazilian government successfully challenged US cotton subsidies at the WTO's Dispute Settlement Body. Al-

WTO Rights Obligation

Jurists debate at length whether the WTO is bound to respect human rights, but in my eyes the answer is a clear yes. Human rights has its place in international law first, because these rights are incumbent on the members of the Organization and because they themselves are bound to fulfil the obligations incumbent on them at an international level.

Next, because the case law of the WTO dispute settlement mechanism acknowledged that international trade law could not be interpreted "in clinical isolation" from international law in general. And, incidentally, how could the WTO—created in 1994 by an international legal instrument—be immune to the rules of the general international law from which it derives its mission and its very existence?

Pascal Lamy, World Trade Organization,
June 5, 2009. www.wto.org.

though the US has not yet reduced these subsidies or compensated Brazilian cotton producers, this decision is already reshaping global cotton markets. Cotton exporters in Chad, Egypt and other countries will directly benefit from this ruling. It may also inspire other developing country governments to challenge such agricultural subsidies. The development organization Oxfam recently noted that developing countries could challenge subsidies for products such as wine, sorghum, and sugar. Over time, if such cases are successful, they may enable more small farmers to obtain their rights to a sustainable livelihood.

WTO rules also require governments to grant producers and consumers new procedural rights. For example, under the

WTO Agreement on Safeguards, a WTO member may take a "safeguard" action (i.e., restrict imports of a product temporarily) to protect a specific domestic industry from an increase in imports of any product which is causing, or threatening to cause, serious injury to the industry. Thus, in the past year, when both Indonesia and Jordan initiated safeguard investigations, both governments gave public notice and held hearings where both domestic and foreign interested parties could respond. In addition, the Customs Valuation Agreement requires governments to legally establish the importer's right to appeal a determination of customs value. And, the Agreement on Technical Barriers to Trade requires governments to publish standards and technical regulations and allow interested parties to comment on them. Taken in sum, these rules have prodded WTO members to be more accountable to their citizens. Over time, these rules may expand the circle of individuals who influence trade policy.

WTO Can Be More Effective

Unfortunately, trade conducted under WTO rules has not always advanced human rights. WTO rules allow many countries to maintain trade distorting subsidies and preferences which may undermine the ability of small manufacturers and farmers to compete in global markets. Moreover, under a WTO waiver, many governments exempt firms from their domestic labor, fiscal and financial rules in their export processing zones. As a result, workers in these zones do not have the same rights as their fellow citizens.

In fact, WTO rules barely mention human rights. While other international organizations such as the UN, the World Bank, and the IMF [International Monetary Fund] have recently announced that they would work to ensure that their efforts and activities promoted human rights, the WTO has not made similar statements.

Additional Measures

WTO members can do more to advance human rights. They should begin by establishing a working group to examine how WTO rules may affect internationally accepted human rights standards, such as those delineated in the Universal Declaration on Human Rights. This group could study how members might use domestic policies such as procurement rules to advance human rights as they seek to expand trade. For example, some European governments want to include adherence to International Labor Organization conventions as selection criteria for the awarding of public contracts. These countries need to know if these actions violate their WTO obligations. Moreover, this working group could examine if the WTO should develop rules for trade in conflict zones. Finally, the working group should examine how the WTO could ensure that members do not undermine workers rights within export processing zones.

The WTO deserves credit for indirectly providing power to more people. Nonetheless, the members of the WTO must do more to ensure that as entities and individuals trade, human rights are not undermined. The public and policymakers can advance human rights at the same time that we expand trade.

"[WTO] negotiations over proposed trade agreements appear to ignore member states' duty to respect human rights."

WTO Actions Can Ignore Human Rights

Amnesty International

Amnesty International is an organization that works to improve human rights around the world. In the following statement, the group expresses its concern that World Trade Organization trade negotiations have virtually ignored human rights concerns. Amnesty International urges greater attention to the human rights of citizens affected by WTO trade agreements as well as more opportunities to improve conditions for all sectors of society, especially the poor and oppressed.

As you read, consider the following questions:

1. How should governments assess the impact of trade agreements on human rights, according to Amnesty International?

2. How do trade-related intellectual property rules impact human rights, in the author's view?

3. Why should Least Developed Countries (LDCs) make full use of the seven-year extension for the compliance with the WTO Agreement on Trade Related Aspects of Intellectual Property Rights (TRIPS)?

As officials of 148 governments prepare [in December 2005] to gather in Hong Kong for the Sixth Ministerial Conference of the World Trade Organization (WTO), Amnesty International [AI] is concerned that negotiations over proposed trade agreements appear to ignore member states' duty to respect human rights.

Denial of Rights

While trade agreements have created new opportunities for some and can have a positive human rights impact, they have also at times been associated with patterns of growing inequality and deteriorating social conditions, including denial of human rights for the poorest and most marginalised sectors of the population.

Assessments of the effects of trade liberalisation have generally concentrated on how they affect countries' overall economic growth. Very little, if any, work has been carried out by governments to assess the potential human rights impact of trade liberalization and in particular to outline what complementary measures are needed to ensure that all sectors of society, including the marginalised, the poor and those who experience systemic discrimination, can benefit from trade agreements.

Human Rights Assessments

All members of the United Nations have pledged under the UN Charter to take both joint and separate action to achieve universal respect for, and observance of, human rights for all without distinction. All governments have a duty to ensure that their actions do not result in the abuse, violation or denial of human rights, including the rights of people in other countries where this is within their sphere of influence. AI believes that, in order to comply with this obligation, all states should undertake comprehensive human rights impact assessments prior to concluding any new trade agreements. Moreover, with regard to all concluded agreements, governments should closely monitor their impact, taking necessary measures to ensure that no-one is unable, for reasons of the impact of trade agreements, to realise their human rights.

These assessments should be undertaken in a manner which recognises the right of the population to participate in the conduct of public affairs, in particular the right of those who are most likely to be affected, the most marginalised. Assessments should be carried out in a manner that ensures that sound empirical evidence is drawn from public, independent and transparent evaluation, based on information gathered through a participatory and consultative process with concerned individuals and including women, minorities, indigenous peoples and other groups facing discrimination.

Intellectual Property Rights

An example of particular concern to Amnesty International is that of stringent trade-related intellectual property rules. The strict enforcement of rules on pharmaceutical patents can and often do hinder access to essential medicines for all. Where trade agreements result in a retrogression in access to essential medicines, governments which implement these agreements risk violating the right to the highest attainable standard of health.

The WTO Agreement on Trade Related Aspects of Intellectual Property Rights (TRIPS) remains problematic in practice for many developing countries despite the adoption of the Doha Declaration [agreements reached during the round of

The Power of Globalization

Globalization is not new. It is a process, not a policy. Historians argue that there were higher levels of trade, and certainly a greater movement of people, one hundred years ago than there are today. What is new is that everyone knows about it, has an opinion, and that is good. The questions of how we manage change is what we are here to discuss. Some think if you abolished the WTO then you would abolish globalization. I believe that the civilized answer to differences is rules and law. What brings the WTO into this debate is our dispute settlement system, which binds outcomes legally. Good people are puzzled. Why, they ask, can we have a binding system for trade but not the for environment, labour, children and gender rights, human rights, animal rights, indigenous rights? Why can we not settle differences that drive nations and tribes to war in a similar way? Good point.

Mike Moore,
World Trade Organization,
July 6, 2001. www.wto.org.

WTO talks begun in 2001 in Doha, Qatar] on TRIPS and Public Health which reaffirms a state's ability to use all the flexibilities in TRIPS in order to reduce the cost of medicines.

The 30 August 2003 General Council decision to implement paragraph 6 of the Doha Declaration on the TRIPS Agreement, aimed at enabling countries without pharmaceutical manufacturing capacity to obtain generic medicines under compulsory license, is viewed by many experts as too cumbersome to adequately resolve the problem of access to medicines for the poor.

Assessment of TRIPS Is Vital

Now that the Least Developed Countries (LDCs) have been granted a seven-year extension to implement TRIPS, it is essential they make full use of the extension by undertaking effective assessments of the impact of proposed intellectual property rules on the enjoyment of human rights and taking necessary legal and other measures to make full use of the agreement's flexibilities.

Amnesty International would urge all leaders of the 148 governments to ensure that human rights obligations are a central consideration during the forthcoming WTO meeting.

In this respect Amnesty International urges all the 148 governments to:

- Ensure LDCs make full use of the seven-year extension for the compliance of the TRIPS obligations.

- Developed countries should cooperate with at least one LDC by helping them to develop their technological base and to conduct, in conjunction with other relevant agencies, a human rights impact assessment to ensure their compliance with the TRIPS obligations will not negatively affect the human rights of their populations.

- Commit to carrying out participatory human rights impact assessment before concluding any new trade agreements, or making revisions to existing ones.

- Ensure that decisions made are informed and complemented by exchanges with governmental bodies responsible for ensuring compliance with human rights obligations. The governments may, for example, consider including at least one human rights expert in their delegations.

- Offer political support to ensure that relevant UN agencies and organizations build on existing expertise and best practice worldwide in order to identify an effective model of human rights impact assessment, which will include the development of appropriate methodology and human rights indicators and benchmarks.

> *"The regulations we enacted under Theodore Roosevelt . . . need to become part of the rules of the World Trade Organization."*

The WTO Can Establish Food Safety Standards

Harold Meyerson

Harold Meyerson is the editor-at-large for the American Prospect *and the* Washington Post. *In the following essay he cites food safety as a growing concern in the United States—especially when much of America's food is being imported from China, which has a poor safety record in that area. Meyerson contends that there is a need for an international organization to assume the duties of establishing food safety on an international scale, and believes that the World Trade Organization is the likely choice for the job.*

As you read, consider the following questions:

1. According to Rick Weiss, as cited by the author, how many foods from China were detained at U.S. ports by the Food and Drug Administration (FDA) in April 2007?

Harold Meyerson, "For a Global FDA," *The American Prospect*, May 24, 2007.

2. What percentage of Chinese food imports do FDA inspectors check, according to Meyerson?

3. What does the author attribute to the founding of the FDA?

And what is madame's dining preference this evening? Scallops coated with putrefying bacteria? Or mushrooms laced with illegal pesticides?

These delicacies and more were among the hundred-plus foods from China that our Food and Drug Administration detained at U.S. ports last month, Rick Weiss reported in Sunday's *Washington Post*. Detained and sent back to the importers, who ofttimes sent them back to us again.

And that's just the hors d'oeuvres. Moving on to the entrée, madame can sup on U.S. chicken, pork, and fish tainted with Chinese pet food ingredients, or on poultry arriving in crates labeled "prune slices" and "vegetables," from Chinese slaughterhouses straight out of Upton Sinclair's 1906 novel, *The Jungle.*

Madame will be happy to know that her government is working to speed more of these toxins to her table. FDA inspectors are able to check less than 1 percent of regulated Chinese food imports (which is why the importers, if at first they don't succeed, try, try again), but the Bush administration is not content to rest on its laurels. Under pressure from U.S. agribusiness, which wants more entry to the Chinese market—something the Chinese will not grant absent more entry to our market—the Agriculture Department is reportedly inclined to change its rules and let China send us its chicken undisguised.

If it does, Weiss reports, much of American business will breathe easier. "So many U.S. companies are directly or indirectly involved in China now," says Robert B. Cassidy, a former assistant U.S. trade representative for China, "the commercial

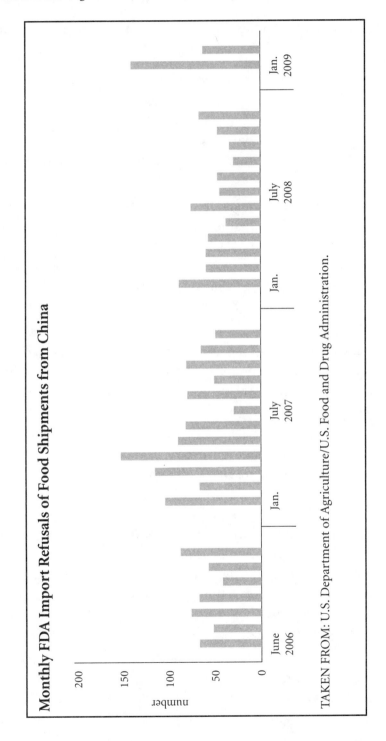

Monthly FDA Import Refusals of Food Shipments from China

TAKEN FROM: U.S. Department of Agriculture/U.S. Food and Drug Administration.

interest of the United States these days has become to allow imports to come in as quickly and smoothly as possible."

Cassidy understates the economic benefits. He omits the boost to our pet-cemetery industry—and for its human counterpart, we can only guess.

Now, you may have missed, in all those impassioned defenses of globalization, the part about uninspected and unregulated food from distant lands showing up, unannounced, for dinner. Yet this was always an implicit part of globalization—at least of the globalization we have today, structured of, by, and for business and financial interests. For globalization was never merely about access to bigger markets than could be found at home. It was also about extending commerce beyond the bounds of regulation and unions and meddlesome meat inspectors.

The incidence of malignant meat imports reaching market can be diminished, I don't doubt, by a greatly expanded FDA. But no one should be deluded that such last-minute interception is remotely equivalent to having our inspectors in the plants. Eating Chungking chicken, if it's really from Chungking, requires a leap of faith that eating Iowa beef, if it's really from Iowa, does not. As Ronald Reagan said of Soviet missiles, so we should say of Chungking chicken: Trust, but verify. The FDA, having no access to China, isn't the best vehicle for verification, and the Chinese food-safety bureaucracy, based on the caliber of Chinese exports, leaves something to be desired, too.

Which is to say, if we're going to globalize the food we eat and wish to be safe, we need to get serious about globalization. The regulations we enacted under Theodore Roosevelt, who established the FDA (partly in response to the outcry Sinclair's novel prompted), need to become part of the rules of the World Trade Organization, which in turn needs real inspectors to enforce those rules. Granted, this is a utopian proposal, but ultimately it is the only sensible response to the borderless business utopia we have now: a global economy devoid of the regulations nations once enacted to protect their citizens when their economies were merely national.

It should come as no surprise if food-safety standards emerge—slowly—as some of the first real global regulations. The FDA was one of the earliest national regulatory agencies—partly because meat crossed state lines (Chicago, recall, was hog butcher to the world), partly because Sinclair's novel made millions of Americans anxious about what they ate. Sinclair had intended his tale of life in a slaughterhouse to spark outrage about the indignities inflicted on meatpackers, but readers couldn't get past his descriptions of the meat. "I aimed for the nation's heart," Sinclair said, "and hit its stomach."

As then, so now: The stomach remains the soft underbelly of the reign of laissez faire. Absent regulations, madame will skip dessert.

> *"The primary goal [of the WTO] is opening borders to facilitate trade and NOT to promote food safety."*

The WTO Is More Interested in Free Trade than Food Safety

Gail Combs

Gail Combs is a chemist and quality engineer. In the following viewpoint, Combs argues that control of food safety has shifted from government to corporate control in the past several years, allowing corporations to rewrite rules and regulations regarding food safety. Combs also notes that the World Trade Organization's international guidelines are a particular problem, as they are more focused on ensuring open and fair international trade and not on the protection of public health.

As you read, consider the following questions:

1. What does the Trade Related Aspects of Intellectual Property Rights (TRIPS) encompass, according to the author?

2. How does the author describe the Codex Alimentarius?

Gail Combs, "Food Safety: Who's Really in Charge Here?" *OpEdNews*, March 9, 2009. Reproduced by permission.

3. According to Combs, how many of the WTO member states include consumer representatives?

Americans are under the false assumption they control US laws through their duly elected officials. This is especially true when it comes to food safety. This used to be the case but in the last decade the balance of power shifted sharply in favor of corporate control of rule making. Corporations have always had a disproportionate amount of power because of money for campaign donations and lobbying. But in 1995 they made a giant leap forward in consolidating their position with the ratification of the World Trade Organization (WTO). A VP of [agriculture giant] Cargill drafted the *Agreement on Agriculture* (AoA) with the agenda of promoting trade at the expense of food safety.

The AoA SPS Agreement [on the Application of Sanitary and Phytosanitary Measures] "*Aims to ensure that governments do not use quarantine and food safety requirements as Unjustified trade barriers.*" This statement shows the primary goal is opening borders to facilitate trade and NOT to promote food safety.

The Codex Alimentarius

The WTO contains several separate agreements, *Trade Related Aspects of Intellectual Property Rights (TRIPS)* introduced patenting of plants, animals and seeds. This allows international corporations to patent genetics stolen from farmers. The crucial agreements for food safety are the *Agreement on the Application of Sanitary and Phytosanitary Measures* (SPS Agreement) and TBT (*Technical Barriers to Trade*). These Agreements designate Codex Alimentarius as a key source of recognized international food standards. WTO considers Codex the international authority for the resolution of disputes. Trade Sanctions can and will be used to enforce compliance. Since World Trade Organization rules apply to over 90 percent of international trade, Trade Sanctions have a lot of bite.

As the WTO matures and its approved international regulatory organizations produce a steady stream of "International Guidelines" WTO intrudes more and more in the internal law of countries compelling them to "harmonize" with the international guidelines. Guidelines with the primary goal of making money for international corporations. . . .

A Closer Look at the Codex

For those who wonder if international guidelines are a problem, let us take a closer look at Codex Alimentarius. Codex's mandate includes ensuring fair international trade in food and protecting the health of consumers. These two competing objectives are sharply different from that of the USDA [U.S. Department of Agriculture] and the FDA [Food and Drug Administration], whose sole mandate was to protect public health. Codex is not subject to a standard requiring it to apply precautionary principles to ensure public health is sufficiently protected. . . .

Problems with the Codex

Codex's voting rules are not conducive to food safety. The standards are adopted by means of one country one vote with the vast majority comprised of votes from developing countries. Countries are not barred from voting on the passage of standards that would promote their respective economic interests at the expense of public health protection.

Codex's standard-setting procedures include the Commission's adoption of certain standards in closed sessions. There is a marked under-representation of consumer and environmental organizations, but industry groups have been closely involved in the Codex standard-setting process for a long time. This imbalance of power is reflected in the composition of member-states' delegations. Many include industry advisors, but only 3 out of the 165 member states (the United States, Germany, and Norway) include consumer representatives.

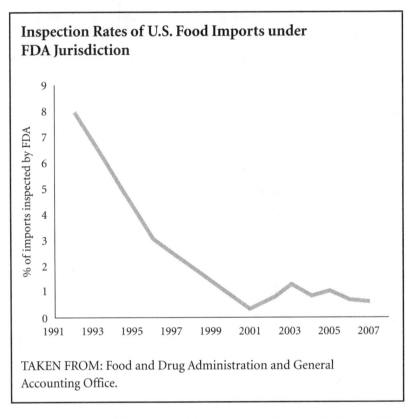

Inspection Rates of U.S. Food Imports under FDA Jurisdiction

TAKEN FROM: Food and Drug Administration and General Accounting Office.

Another problem is WTO mandated "scientific" and "risk based" guidelines. These guidelines are based on corporate or corporate-sponsored research. Since industry now funds most university research any unfavorable research is likely to be suppressed. Therefore Codex can say genetically modified foods and certain chemical additives are OK and should not be subject to restriction or labeling, while vitamins and food supplements must have strict guidelines limiting dosage.

The Blame Game

In the House and Senate there are now WTO/Corporate sponsored bills that will eliminate competition and shift liability from corporate production facilities to local farmers. Corporation lawyers are already drawing up contracts placing all blame for food safety problems squarely on the farmer. There are even seminars being given on "limiting risk and safe guarding stockholder assets in the event of recalls" so everyone in industry uses the same type of contract to shift liability to farmers.

Where is the USA today? The *WORLD TRADE REPORT 2005 C* sums it up best. The USDA and FDA are busy restructuring "the safest food system in the world" to comply with food standards acceptable to Ag Corporations who want to make money exporting food of dubious quality from third world nations and cheap tax supported grain from first world countries.

> The overview suggests that the standards development process organized by national, regional and international standards institutions is progressively evolving. The role of international bodies has gained prominence. The national standardization infrastructures of most industrialized countries are now integrated into the network of international standardization. In Europe, for instance, adoption of European standards is mandatory for national member bodies and European standards organizations transpose the international standards into European standards.

In 2007 [U.S. president George W.] Bush signed an agreement with the EU [European Union] "*. . . to push ahead with regulatory convergence in nearly 40 areas . . .*" So, Who's really in charge here?

Periodical Bibliography

Ronald Bailey   "Perpetuating Poverty by Protecting
                                 Livelihoods," *Reason*, August 5, 2008.

Doug Bandow   "Playing Geoeconomics in Asia," *American
                                 Spectator*, January 18, 2007.

Thomas E. Brewton   "Free-Trade Hypocrisy," *Intellectual
                                 Conservative*, April 30, 2007.

Center for   "Trading Up Through Multilateralism," March
American Progress   21, 2007.

Edwin J. Feulner   "U.S. Needs to Keep Up the Fight Against
                                 Trade Barriers," Heritage Foundation, August 3,
                                 2006. www.heritage.org.

Daniel T. Griswold   "Globalization, Human Rights, and
                                 Democracy," Cato Institute, August 11, 2006.

Michael Hudson   "Financing the Empire," *Counterpunch*, May 30,
                                 2009.

Daniel Ikenson   "Trade, Growth: Weep Not for Doha," Cato
                                 Institute, July 20, 2008. www.cato.org.

Andrew Leonard   "South Korean Farmers: The WTO's Most
                                 Lethal Enemy," *Salon*, December 12, 2005.
                                 www.salon.com.

Melinda Liu   "Power Up," *Newsweek*, September 7, 2009.

John Nichols   "Bush's Globalization Drive Crashes . . . Again,"
                                 Nation, July 29, 2008.

John Nichols   "The World and Pittsburgh," *Nation*,
                                 September 16, 2009.

Michael Schuman   "Potholes on the Path to Prosperity," *Time*,
                                 February 2, 2009.

Barrett Sheridan   "The Myths of Recession," *Newsweek*, February
                                 14, 2009.

OPPOSING
VIEWPOINTS®
SERIES

CHAPTER 2

Is the World Trade Organization Essential to U.S. Interests?

Chapter Preface

The Doha Development Round, or the Doha Development Agenda (DDA), is the name for the most recent round of World Trade Organization (WTO) trade negotiations. Commencing in November 2001 with a ministerial-level meeting in Doha, Qatar, the Doha Round aimed to lower trade barriers around the world, especially for developing countries trying to establish free trade relationships with developed countries. Subsequent meetings in the Doha Round have occurred in Cancun, Mexico, in 2003 and Hong Kong in 2005. Related negotiations also took place in Geneva, Switzerland, in 2004, 2006, and 2008; Paris in 2005; and Potsdam, Germany, in 2007.

From the beginning of the Doha Round, trade negotiations ran into problems. Talks stalled over disagreements on several major issues, including agriculture, industrial tariffs and non-tariff barriers, services, and trade remedies. The most serious conflict—and the one that threatened to subvert the Doha Round—was the tension between developed nations, led by the European Union, the United States, and Japan, and key developing countries represented by India, Brazil, China, and South Africa. Another significant conflict that arose during the Doha Round was between the European Union and the United States over their agricultural barriers, which operate effectively as trade barriers.

The Doha Round derailed during the most recent round of trade negotiations in Geneva, which took place July 23–29, 2008. The talks collapsed when India and the United States were in dispute over the special safeguard mechanism (SSM), a measure designed to protect poor farmers from an unexpected import surge or price collapse by imposing a special tariff on the imports of certain goods. As negotiations broke down, countries pointed fingers at each other, blaming each other for the Doha collapse.

However, calls to renew negotiations quickly started. In 2009 at the G20 summit of the top twenty world leaders, a declaration included a pledge to complete the Doha Round. Certainly, plans are being made to meet again to try to make progress on the most difficult issues facing the WTO and the global trading system.

Some critics of the WTO and free trade applaud the breakdown of the Doha Round, decrying the negotiations as unfair to the United States or to developing countries like India or Brazil. They find the entire negotiation process as it stands as inherently unfair; however, supporters argue that the Doha Round is essential to American interests and it is therefore imperative to revive negotiations and make significant progress on relevant trade issues.

The viewpoints in the following chapter debate whether the WTO is essential to U.S. trade interests and the relationship between the WTO and the U.S. manufacturing industry.

| "The WTO exists as the most important
vehicle to advance U.S. trade interests."

The WTO Is Essential to U.S. Economic Interests

Peter F. Allgeier

Peter F. Allgeier is a deputy U.S. trade representative. In the following testimony before the Subcommittee on Trade of the Committee on Ways and Means of the House of Representatives, he enumerates the reasons the World Trade Organization facilitates U.S. trade interests and benefits the U.S. economy. Allgeier urges continued U.S. participation in the WTO in order to stay competitive in the global economy.

As you read, consider the following questions:

1. How many nations belong to the WTO, as cited by the author?

2. According to Allgeier, what countries are participating in ongoing negotiations for WTO membership?

3. How much have U.S. exports of goods and services increased in the first ten years of existence of the WTO (1994–2004), according to the author?

Peter F. Allgeier, "The Future of the World Trade Organization," Hearing Before the Subcommittee on Trade of the Committee on Ways and Means, House of Representatives, May 17, 2005.

I am pleased to be here to discuss the World Trade Organization (WTO) and the WTO Agreements, the relationship to the strategic and economic interests of the United States, and the overwhelming value of continued U.S. participation in the WTO. . . .

My testimony today provides an opportunity to look back at the creation of the WTO and our participation over the last 10 years and, equally important, to focus on our agenda for the next several months leading up to the Sixth WTO Ministerial in Hong Kong this December [2005] and head toward a successful conclusion of the Doha Development Agenda negotiations in 2006.

Historical Context for the WTO

The creation of the WTO represented the culmination of a decades-long bipartisan U.S. commitment to lead the world away from economic isolationism and toward the imperative of an open, rules-based global trading system. The GATT [General Agreement on Tariffs and Trade] had been created in 1947—drawn up in an unsteady post-war world that collectively was determined to strengthen global security and peace through economic opportunity and growth in living standards.

Today, we continue to exercise our leadership in a world that faces new challenges to maintaining global security and stability, underscoring the continuing important strategic interest of the United States in an open global trading system governed by the rule of law. The United States is fully engaged in the WTO work under the Doha Development Agenda, and the United States aggressively uses the existing WTO machinery to effectively enforce our rights.

WTO membership now stands at 148. Accession to the WTO carries more stringent requirements than what was used in the GATT. Key entries during the past decades include not only China, but also a wide array of other countries that each carry their own strategic and economic importance, such as Jordan, Cambodia, and several former Soviet Republics. Negotiations toward entry into the WTO are ongoing at various stages for more than 25 countries, ranging from Russia and Vietnam, to Iraq, Ukraine, Saudi Arabia, and Afghanistan. Each effort underscores the importance attached to membership in the WTO, and the importance of moving forward with a member-driven, rules-based approach to the global trading system.

Commercial Significance

During the five years since the last review under the Uruguay Round Agreements Act [in 2000], unprecedented growth in trade and global economic integration has continued—led by continuing advances in technology, communications, manufacturing, and logistics. Five years ago we did not have ubiquitous cell phones that captured and transmitted photos miles away, nor was it yet routine to use the Internet to order overnight delivery of a product from thousands of miles away. Advances such as these demonstrate that the trade environment is always changing, the citizens of the United States—like the rest of the world—are being presented with new products, new services and, most important, new economic opportunities that did not exist in 1995, or 2000. At the same time, globalization also undoubtedly presents new issues, new competitive challenges and new economic pressures.

Simply put, the WTO exists as the most important vehicle to advance U.S. trade interests, and is critical to America's workers, businesses, farmers, and ranchers. Many are dependent and all are affected by a global trading system that must operate with predictability and transparency, without discrimination against American products, and providing for actions to address unfair trade practices. The United States remains the world's largest exporter. During the first 10 years of the WTO—from 1994 to 2004—U.S. exports of goods and services have risen 63 percent, from $703 billion to over $1.1 trillion.

The WTO Benefits the United States

To ensure equal opportunities for U.S. businesses, farmers, ranchers, and other exporters, the United States has brought more WTO dispute settlement cases than any other member. Since establishment of the WTO, the United States has initiated 74 cases. Examples of cases include those focusing on: dairy, apples, biotechnology; telecommunications, automobiles, apparel, unfair customs procedures, and protecting intellectual property rights. Of those, we have won 23 on core issues, lost four, and settled 23 before decision. The remaining 24 are "in process" (in panel, in consultations, or monitored for progress or otherwise inactive). In the last five years, our record to-date in cases—both offensive and defensive—is 16 wins and 14 losses. From 1995 to 2000, the U.S. record was 18 wins and 15 losses. The United States represents roughly 17 percent of world trade, yet has brought nearly 22 percent of the WTO disputes between January 1, 1995, and December 31, 2004.

This year [2005] marks the full implementation of many key Uruguay Round agreements, such as completion of the 10 year phased implementation of global tariff cuts on industrial and agricultural goods and reductions in trade-distorting agricultural domestic support and export subsidies; elimination of quotas and full integration of textile trade into the multilateral trading system; and improvements in patent protection in key markets such as India. The Uruguay Round was highlighted by the negotiating results being adopted in a "single undertaking" by all Members, who together rejected any notion of a two- or three-tier global trading system.

The WTO also provides opportunities on a day-to-day basis for advancing U.S. interests through the more than 20

United States

Basic Indicators

Population (thousands, 2007)	301,621
GDP (million current US$, 2007)	13,811,200
Trade per capita (US$, 2005–2007)	11,954
Trade to GDP ratio (2005–2007)	27.2

Rank in world trade, 2007	Exports	Imports
Merchandise	3	1
Commercial services	1	1

TAKEN FROM: *WTO Trade Profiles 2008.*

---

standing WTO Committees—not including numerous additional Working Groups, Working Parties, and Negotiating Bodies—which meet regularly to administer agreements, for Members to exchange views, work to resolve questions of Members' compliance with commitments, and develop initiatives aimed to improve the agreements and their operation.

Greater Transparency in WTO

The United States has advocated greater transparency and openness in WTO proceedings. The WTO has taken important steps to increase the transparency of its operation across the board, from document availability to public outreach. WTO Members continue to set the course for the organization, and the Members themselves remain responsible for compliance with rules.

Responding to U.S. leadership, during the past 10 years the WTO has shown itself to be a dynamic organization, one where our interests are advanced toward achievements with concrete positive effect. We have seen to it that the substantive agenda has provided the path for significant market-opening results over the past decade, such as concluding the Information Technology Agreement (ITA) to eliminate tariffs worldwide on IT products, and bringing the Basic Telecommunications Agreement into effect, which opened up 95 percent of the world's telecommunications markets. Both are achievements that continue to contribute to the ability of citizens around the globe to take advantage of the Information Age.

The 1997 Agreement on Trade in Financial Services has achieved fair, open and transparent practices across the global financial services industry, fostering a climate of greater global economic security. The agreement helps ensure that U.S. banking, securities insurance, and other financial services firms can compete and invest in overseas markets on clear and fair terms.

Essential to U.S. Interests

In a world where over 95 percent of consumers live beyond our borders, the WTO is an essential tool for U.S. interests. Increasingly, small businesses are important players in the global economy and an important stake holder in advancing U.S. interests in the WTO agenda. Between 1992 and 2002, U.S. exports from small and medium-sized enterprises rose 54 percent, from $102.8 billion to $158.5 billion—a faster pace than the rate of growth for total U.S. exports during the same time.

Falling trade barriers—many of which reflect the 10 year implementation of the results of the Uruguay Round—have helped rapidly increase the value of trade relative to the U.S. economy. U.S. goods and service trade (exports plus imports) reached the levels of 18 percent of the value of U.S. GDP [gross domestic product] in 1984, 21.7 percent in 1994 and 25.2 percent in 2004. Both U.S. manufacturing exports and U.S. agricultural exports have grown strongly during our 10 years in the WTO. Between 1994 and 2004, they were up 65 percent and 38 percent, respectively. U.S. exports of high technology products grew by 67 percent during the past 10 years and accounted for one-quarter of total goods exports.

During this time period, U.S. exports to Mexico more than doubled, while exports to Canada and the EU [European Union] grew by 66 percent and 56 percent, respectively. Among major countries and regions, exports to China exhibited the fastest growth, nearly quadrupling over the past 10 years. China's entry into the WTO in December 2001 locked in improved market access opportunities, committing to reduce its tariffs on industrial products, which averaged 24.6 percent, to a level that averages 9.4 percent. The growth in services exports between 1994 and 2004 (69 percent) slightly exceeded that of goods (61 percent). Nearly all of the major services export categories have grown between 1994 and 2004.

| "The United States should give notice of withdrawal from the World Trade Organization."

The WTO Works Against U.S. Economic Interests

Ernest F. Hollings

Ernest F. Hollings is a former U.S. senator from South Carolina and former chair of both the Budget and the Commerce committees. In the following viewpoint, he provides a brief history of U.S. trade, claiming that the country has been built on managed trade, or protectionism. Hollings argues that the U.S. government must protect the U.S. economy by reversing our free trade policies under the World Trade Organization and North American Free Trade Agreement (NAFTA) and implementing a more protectionist trade system that would save U.S. jobs.

As you read, consider the following questions:

1. How did the admission of China to the WTO affect the U.S. workforce, according to the author?

2. How many American companies does Hollings say have been lost to foreign control from 1996 to 2006?

Ernest F. Hollings, "We Need Alexander Hamilton," *The American Prospect*, March 7, 2006. Reproduced by permission of the author.

3. According to the author, how many American jobs have been lost under NAFTA?

People now realize that corporate America is blind to the nation's security and its economy. Only government can protect our manufacturers, our economic strength. The bubble of "free trade," and of "protectionism," has popped. The charades of the "trade war" and of "globalization" are over. As [U.S. statesman] Henry Clay observed in 1832, "The call for free trade is as unavailing as the cry of a spoiled child, in its nurse's arms. . . . It never has existed; it never will exist."

Brief History of U.S. Trade

We started a "trade war" when Alexander Hamilton rebuffed Britain's proposal that the freed colony should trade what it produced best while Britain would trade what it produced best—[English economist] David Ricardo's "Doctrine of Comparative Advantage." In his famous "Report on Manufacturers," Hamilton told the Brits to bug off. We are not going to remain your colony, trading our rice, cotton, indigo for your finished goods. We will become a nation-state by building our own manufacture. The first bill to pass Congress on July 4, 1789, was for the seal of the United States. The second bill was a 50-percent tariff on numerous articles. The United States was built on managed trade or protectionism. Abraham Lincoln managed trade for steel for the intercontinental railroad; Franklin Roosevelt managed trade for agriculture; Dwight Eisenhower for oil; John Kennedy for textiles; Ronald Reagan for semiconductors.

By the time of Teddy Roosevelt, Edwin Morris in *Theodore Rex* writes: "This first year of the new century found her (U.S.) worth $25 billion dollars more than her nearest rival, Great Britain, with a gross national product more than twice that of Germany and Russia. The United States was already so rich in goods and services that she was more self-sustaining than any industrial power . . . More than half the world's cotton, corn, copper, and oil flowed from the American cornucopia, and at least one third of all steel, iron, silver, and gold . . . the excellence of her manufactured products guaranteed her dominance of world markets." This industrial might—personified by Rosie the Riveter—was a principal force for victory in World War II. At the end of the War, the United States had the world's only manufacture and wisely launched the Marshall Plan to develop manufacture in Europe and the Pacific Rim. We called for "free trade" in an effort to open markets. But Japan and South Korea's markets remained closed. Even our winking at dumping violations and transshipments failed to budge Japan and South Korea. Now China follows suit.

Recent U.S. Trade History

In recent years, Congress strained to protect the nation's manufacture. It passed four textile bills, with Jimmy Carter vetoing one, Reagan vetoing two, and George H.W. Bush vetoing the fourth. Corporate America got the message: Our standard of living and domestic production were not to be protected—head offshore. By the time of the [Bill] Clinton administration, the nation was not only losing hard manufacture but service jobs. With this outsourcing, candidate Bill Clinton campaigned on protecting the workforce of America with the slogan "it's the economy, stupid." After his inauguration, Clinton, who had been lukewarm about NAFTA [North American Free Trade Agreement] with Mexico during the campaign, surprised everyone with his zeal for it. NAFTA with Canada provided free trade because Canada and the United States have the same standard of living. But Mexico needed to develop a free market for free trade—one including labor rights, property rights, a respected judiciary—in other words, the common market approach. In Europe, before admitting Greece and Portugal to the Common Market, the Market countries taxed themselves some $5 billion over five years to develop in those countries the conditions for a free market. Instead, NAFTA with Mexico protected corporate rights to produce, in disregard for labor, the environment, and the government.

Clinton placed the white tent on the White House lawn for the Fortune 500 and twisted arms to change the vote in Congress, joining congressmen in golf, granting C-17 [cargo plane] contracts, cultural centers, and so on. This had the Democratic Party abandoning labor for corporate America. With the Democratic Leadership Council tending to corporate America, the multinationals, now transnationals, had a free run of government. Textile quotas were terminated, the Glass-Steagall Act [on banking reform] was repealed, and offshore profits were repatriated at a reduced rate. Industry's Man of the Year, Jack Welch, announced that General Electric would not contract with any U.S. subcontractor that had not moved to Mexico. "Squeeze the lemon" was his slogan. Clinton led the way to give "most favored nation status" to China and put China in the World Trade Organization. The WTO pact, a 25,000-page document undermining trade, dumping, and environmental laws, provided an appeal to an unelected tribunal appointed by the transnationals and their consultants. Senator Robert Dole from Kansas realized that this would leave U.S. production "in the hands of the philistines." He attempted to replace the appellate panel with a panel of three federal judges, but the transnationals turned him back. The final blow to the United States workforce came with the admission of China to the WTO. Outsourcing hemorrhaged. Seven hundred-fifty research and development centers sprouted up in China to take advantage of the inexpensive talent pool. Microsoft is doubling its basic lab researchers this year [2006] to 800 full-time scientists. Two-and-a-half trillion dollars has been added to the national debt in the last five years. And [President] George W. Bush now estimates a federal budget deficit this year of

$706 billion. Foreigners have been financing a majority of this debt. Now these dollars flow back in as foreigners gobble up the production of the United States. Eighty-six hundred American companies, at a cost of $1.3 trillion, have been lost to foreign control in the last 10 years.

NAFTA and Its Consequences

NAFTA with Mexico was supposed to create 200,000 U.S. jobs. Instead, we lost 400,000. NAFTA was supposed to limit immigration, but subsidized American agriculture put 2 million Mexican farmers out of business—farmers who later headed for the U.S. border. Even the Mexican industrial worker makes less today than before NAFTA. The U.S. trade deficit [in 2005] was $725.8 billion. The United States lost 2.8 million manufacturing jobs in the last five years. The growth of the U.S. labor force has also slowed. Had it continued at its normal rate, unemployment today would be 6.8 percent, instead of 4.8 percent. The Bureau of Labor Statistics reports that our workforce is so depleted that with two-and-a-half times the population, today we work less manufacturing hours than we worked when Japan hit Pearl Harbor. The Defense Department had to wait for Japan to furnish flat-panel displays so that we could attack [Iraqi dictator] Saddam Hussein during Desert Storm. Our defenses are down. The middle class disappears. Democracy weakens. The country is going out of business.

To open Jones Manufacturing in the United States, Mr. Jones must provide a minimum wage, Social Security, Medicare, Medicaid, clean air, clean water, a safe working place, safe machinery, plant-closing notice, parental leave, and labor rights; he must also comply with equal pay, age discrimination, disability, and anti-trust laws. Our standard of living is a cost of doing business. Today, Jones can go to China, which provides the factory and labor force for 58 cents an hour and none of the cost of doing business in the United States. If

---

"In general, do you think that free trade agreements—like NAFTA, and the policies of the World Trade Organization—have been a good thing or a bad thing for the United States?"

Good thing	Bad thing	Unsure
%	%	%
35	48	17

TAKEN FROM: Pew Research Center/Council on Foreign Relations survey conducted April 23–27, 2008.

Jones's competition outsources to China, and Jones continues to work his own people, Jones Manufacture will go bankrupt. Our problem is that the United States will go bankrupt unless we move to protect Jones Manufacture—to protect our economy. In trade, we have a comparative disadvantage.

Protecting U.S. Security

The security of the United States is like a three-legged stool. The first leg, values, is solid. The world knows of the American stance for freedom and human rights. The second, military is unquestioned. The United States is the world's superpower. But the third leg—economic—has been fractured since the Cold War. We intentionally gave up our production and market to defeat communism. Instead of repairing the fracture at "the fall of the [Berlin] wall," we responded to the call of "free trade." In the beginning, we were told that free trade was the way to open markets—without tariffs or barriers, the United States would open markets for its vast production, increasing jobs. But when jobs and manufacturing were lost, we were told: "Don't fret, the United States is moving from hard manufacture to a service economy." Filthy smokestacks were for other countries. When service jobs hemorrhaged to India, the transnationals then cried "free trade" for high technology and higher paying jobs. Then, with a deficit in the balance of hi-tech trade with China, the scavengers of our economic strength shout: "Globalization—the world is flat!" "One can produce anything, anywhere. Globalization costs jobs but the consumer is rewarded with lower prices. The United States must compete with education. We need engineers." But there are no jobs for the educated, or for engineers. China graduates 350,000 engineers a year, and American industry is outsourcing engineering jobs as fast as it can to India. George W. Bush has just returned from India pledging U.S. nuclear power that will accelerate outsourcing to India. Moreover, the Thailand doctor performs the same operation at one-eighth the cost of the American doctor. And high-tech jobs in this country are being filled with H1-B Visas [allowing foreigners to work].

Ordinarily, business would be hounding politicians to protect the economy, to protect their production, to protect the workforce that it depends on. But today, business doesn't depend on the workforce in the United States. To protect U.S. production in China and India, the Big Banks, the Business Round Table, the Conference Board, the National Association of Manufacturers, the U.S. Retail Association, the U.S. Federation of Independent Business, the U.S. Chamber of Commerce all shout, "Free trade, globalization!" Free trade is a fraud! Globalization is a fraud! With anything produced anywhere, with the satellite transferring money and technology, with Internet monitoring of global production, a country couldn't "erect a wall" or start a "trade war" if it tried. The Big Bank crowd, the Business Roundtable, and the rest, are a "fifth column" in today's "trade war," while the president and Congress are AWOL [absent without leave: deserters].

Government Must Protect the Economy

The government will have to protect the economy. Unfortunately, both the Republican and Democratic parties in Congress are in a race for campaign contributions. The "fifth column" has the money. The money party, Republican, leads the cheer for "free trade!" and "globalization!" The working man's party, Democrat, stands quietly by, begging. Legislation goes wanting.

First, we need to stop financing the elimination of jobs. Tax benefits for offshore production must end. Royalty deductions allowed for offshore activities must be eliminated, and offshore tax havens must be closed down. Next, we need an assistant attorney general to enforce our trade laws and agreements. Currently, enforcement is left to the injured party. It takes corporate America years to jump the legal hurdles. At the end, the president, under his authority for the nation's security, cancels the court order against the trade violation. Rather than waste time and money, corporate America moves offshore. Trade policy is set by a dozen departments and agencies. Policy should be reconstituted in a Department of Trade and Commerce with the secretary acting as a czar. Then trade treaties can be negotiated for the good of the U.S. economy, instead of for the good of the transnational. The department's International Trade Administration, finding a dumping violation, should also determine the penalty. The International Trade Commission should be eliminated. Custom agents charged with drug enforcement and homeland security are hard-pressed to stop trade transshipments. We need 1,000 more Customs agents. We need more funding for research in physical and mathematical sciences and engineering; more funding for the Manufactures Extension Partnership Act and the Advanced Technology Program. The list of materials critical to our national defense should be enforced. H1-B Visas should be repealed, and the United States should give notice of withdrawal from the World Trade Organization.

Finally, competition in world trade today is not for profit, but market share. The closed markets of Japan, South Korea, and China enable exports at cost with the necessary profit being made up in the closed domestic market. A Lexus selling for $33,000 in the United States sells for $47,000 in Japan.

Corporate America's rush to produce for profit in China is a losing game for the nation. Countries winning market share will come to control the market, which is happening now with automotive production in the United States. This production capacity furnished the tanks and planes for WWII. Akio Morita, founder of Sony Corporation, admonished Third World countries to develop a manufacturing capacity to become a nation-state. He then cautioned: "That world power that loses its manufacturing capacity will cease to be a world power."

The United States must stop so-called free trade agreements merely to protect offshore production—and start trading, opening up closed markets, and rebuilding the country.

> *"Policymakers in the U.S. and around the world need to commit to getting [Doha Round] multilateral trade talks back on track in the World Trade Organization."*

The Success of the Doha Development Round Is Essential to U.S. Economic Interests

Daniella Markheim

Daniella Markheim is a senior trade policy analyst in the Center for International Trade and Economics at the Heritage Foundation, a conservative Washington, D.C., think tank. In the following viewpoint, she argues that free trade policy is important in helping the global economy grow and views the success of the WTO's Doha Round of trade negotiations as crucial to this effort. Developing countries, especially, are in line to benefit from the policies being negotiated in the Doha Round, Markheim maintains.

Daniella Markheim, "The Importance of Reviving the Doha Round," *Heritage Foundation Web Memo*, no. 2123, November 5, 2008. Reproduced by permission.

As you read, consider the following questions:

1. What does the author refer to when she discusses "deadlocked" issues?

2. According to Markheim, what has been the average of real growth in goods and services among lower-income and lower-middle-income countries since 1995?

3. Trade integration in lower-income and lower-middle-income countries has raised from 71 percent in the early 1990s to what percentage in 2008, according to the author?

Overlooked in the daily onslaught of negative global financial and economic news—not to mention campaign rhetoric—is the vital and positive role that international trade and open markets have played in helping companies stay afloat in today's tough economic climate. America's free trade policies—that favorite bugaboo of protectionists on both sides of the political aisle—and a relatively open investment regime have cushioned the U.S. economy as domestic consumers and investors have tightened their purse strings and cashed out their mutual funds. Now that the economic storm has spread from the U.S. to much of the world, the need to keep the nation's trade and investment barriers low and competitive is even more critical.

With many countries' economic well-being linked through trade and investment, the need for all nations to embrace trade and investment liberalization is crucial to helping the global economy recover and grow. Sadly, rather than calmly assessing what policies are needed to restore confidence in U.S. and world financial markets, politicians everywhere are stumbling over each other to design interventionist schemes that could reverse many hard-won and beneficial open market policies—policies that many leaders are wrongly blaming today's economic turmoil on precisely such interventionist policies. Rather than panicking or pandering to special interests, policymakers in the U.S. and around the world need to commit to getting multilateral trade talks back on track in the World Trade Organization and should remain vigilant against implementing protectionist investment policies as important elements to any long-term economic recovery strategy.

The Doha Round

As its name implies, the current Doha Development Round of multilateral trade negotiations was founded on the principle of promoting economic development along with freer trade. Member nations, developed and developing alike, went into the negotiations with the idea that any new agreement would result in developing countries being better integrated with and benefiting from the global economy.

When a country lowers its barriers to trade, it opens its economy to competition and a wider variety of goods and services than was previously available. Competition spurs the movement of labor and capital from industries that cannot compete to those that can, enabling the country to both produce more efficiently and attract new investment—critical elements of any long-term development strategy. Of course, freer trade also means that exporters can sell their products in more countries' markets. However, for a country trying to develop its economy, merely gaining additional access to wealthy markets is not enough to spur the same kind of momentum needed for sustainable growth as the efficient use of resources and new inflows of investment.

In that regard, one of the biggest boosts to freer trade and sustainable development would come not only from developed countries making meaningful progress on dismantling remaining trade barriers but also from developing countries making binding commitments under the Doha Round to reduce what are some of the world's highest tariffs and other trade barriers against the developed world. Yet even more critically, developed countries must reduce tariffs and other barriers to trade against each other. The IMF [International Monetary Fund] reports that manufacturing tariffs in developing countries are four times higher than in developed countries, and separate research has determined that 70 percent of tariffs paid by developing countries go to other developing countries.

Dead-Locked Issues

Rather than highlighting broad disagreement over what a comprehensive multilateral trade agreement should look like, the collapse of global trade negotiations in July of [2008] reflected the inability of countries to agree on a handful of "dead-locked" issues. Of particular concern was the demand that developing countries be granted an excessive special safeguard mechanism as a means to protect domestic producers from import surges. Had this demand been fulfilled, developing countries would have been able to apply higher, temporary tariffs in excess of current bound rates, undermining not only the fundamental objective of negotiating for freer trade but also reversing progress made earlier under the Uruguay Round and in the accession agreements defining the trade liberalizing commitments of newer members.

Such a reversal of progress would have a tangible impact on rich developing and developed countries alike. For example, since the WTO was established in 1995, real growth in trade of goods and services among lower-income and lower-middle-income countries has averaged more than 7.5 percent, while high-income countries have experienced 7.2 percent average growth—faster on average than these countries' average rate of GDP [gross domestic product] growth. With countries trading more, it is no surprise that they are more integrated with the global economy. Measured by the ratio of trade to GDP, lower-income and lower-middle-income countries' trade integration rose from an average 71 percent in the early 1990s

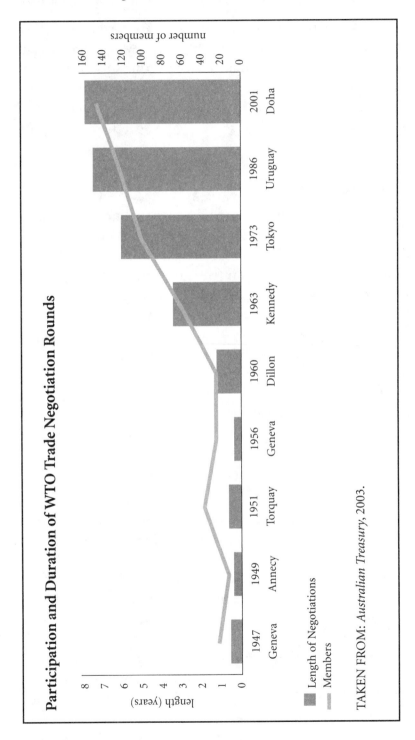

Participation and Duration of WTO Trade Negotiation Rounds

number of members

length (years)

| 1947 Geneva | 1949 Annecy | 1951 Torquay | 1956 Geneva | 1960 Dillon | 1963 Kennedy | 1973 Tokyo | 1986 Uruguay | 2001 Doha |

Length of Negotiations
Members

TAKEN FROM: *Australian Treasury*, 2003.

to 94 percent today. Trade integration increased for high-income countries as well, climbing from an average 113 percent to 132 percent. With international trade playing an increasing role in the economic performance of nations and countries becoming ever more connected to global markets, the cost of backtracking on the commitments WTO members have already made would not only result in a slower recovery from today's economic slump, but it would also undermine efforts to advance economic development.

Reduce Barriers to Trade

There is nothing wrong with developing countries taking extra time to implement trade reforms, especially when these countries are clearly striving to introduce broad policy changes as part of a comprehensive reform of their economic policies and institutions. However, the overarching goal of the trade talks is to reduce barriers to trade, not erect more of them. International trade has been a source of growth for all participants, and WTO members need to make meaningful contributions towards an agreement—if one is to be had. Nations can strike the biggest blow against poverty and achieve a faster pace of economic recovery by helping to conclude the Doha Round with an agreement that eliminates trade-distorting policies in all countries, rich or poor. And the faster the pace of trade liberalization, the better. After all, doggedly holding on to protectionist trade policies for as long as possible only further delays economic development.

| "The collapse of World Trade Organiza-
tion negotiations '... is a very painful
failure.'"

The Doha Development Negotiations Are a Failure

Robert Weissman

Robert Weissman is editor of the Multinational Monitor *and director of* Essential Action. *In the following viewpoint, he notes
the breakdown of the Doha Round of World Trade Organization
trade negotiations, maintaining that the proposed trade policies
were inherently unfair to developing countries.*

As you read, consider the following questions:

1. What did the Doha Round promise to developing countries, according to the author?

2. What does Weissman believe caused the breakdown of
   the Doha Round?

3. Why does the author believe that there was so little support for the Doha Round in both rich and poor countries?

Robert Weissman, "The Collapse of the WTO Talks," *Counterpunch*, July 31, 2008. Reproduced by permission.

Predictably, the cheerleaders for corporate globalization are bemoaning the collapse of World Trade Organization negotiations.

"This is a very painful failure and a real setback for the global economy when we really needed some good news," said Peter Mandelson, the European Union's trade commissioner.

Even worse, says the corporate globalization rah-rah crowd, the talks' failure will hurt the developing world. After all, these negotiations were named the Doha Development Round.

"The breakdown of these talks is bad news for the world's businesses, workers, farmers and most importantly the poor," laments U.S. Chamber of Commerce President Tom Donohue.

Doha Was Unfair

But don't shed any tears for the purported beneficiaries of the WTO talks. If truth-in-advertising rules applied, this might have been called the Doha Anti-Development Round.

The alleged upside of the deal for developing countries—increased access to rich country markets—would have been of tiny benefit, even according to the World Bank. The Research and Information System for Developing Countries points out that Bank analyses showed a successful conclusion of the Doha Round would, by 2015, increase developing country income in total by $16 billion a year—less than a penny a day for every person in the developing world.

The World Bank study, however, includes numerous questionable assumptions, without which developing countries would emerge as net losers. One unrealistic assumption is that governments will make up for lost tariff revenues by other forms of taxes. Another is that countries easily adjust to import surges by depreciating their currencies and increasing exports.

In any case, the important point is that there was very little to gain for developing countries.

By contrast, there was a lot to lose.

Doha Did Not Add Up

The promise to developing countries was that they would benefit from reduced agricultural tariffs and subsidies in the rich countries. Among developing nations, these gains would have been narrowly concentrated among Argentina, Brazil and a few other countries with industrial agriculture.

What the spike in food prices has made clear to developing countries is that their food security depends fundamentally not on cheap imports, but on enhancing their capacity to feed themselves. The Doha rules would have further undermined this capacity.

"Opening of markets, removal of tariffs and withdrawal of state intervention in agriculture has turned developing countries from net food exporters to net food importers and burdened them with huge import bills," explains food analyst Anuradha Mittal of the Oakland Institute. "This process, which leaves the poor dependent on uncertain and volatile global markets for their food supply, has wiped out millions of livelihoods and placed nearly half of humanity at the brink of hunger and starvation."

Farmers' movements around the world delivered this message to government negotiators, and the negotiators refused to cave to the aggressive demands made by rich countries on behalf of agricultural commodity-trading multinationals. Kamal Nath, India's Minister for Commerce and Industry, pointed out that the Doha Development Round was supposed to give benefits to developing countries—especially in agriculture—not extract new concessions.

Cause of Collapse

The immediately proximate cause of the negotiations' collapse was a demand by developing countries that they maintain effective tools to protect themselves from agricultural import surges. Rich countries refused the overly modest demand.

"WTO-Free Traitor," by Glen Foden. www.cartoonstock.com.

And agriculture was the area where developing countries were going to benefit.

The rough trade at the heart of the deal was supposed to be that rich countries reduce market barriers to developing country agricultural exports, and developing countries further open up to rich country manufacturing and service exports and investment.

Such a deal "basically suggests that the poor countries should remain agricultural forever," says Ha-Joon Chang, an economics professor at the University of Cambridge and author of *Bad Samaritans: The Myth of Free Trade and the Secret History of Capitalism.* "In order to receive the agricultural concession, the developing countries basically have to abolish their industrial tariffs and other means to promote industrialization." In other words, he says, developing countries are supposed to forfeit the tools that almost every industrialized country (and the successful Asian manufacturing exporters) has used to build their industrial capacity.

A Lose-Lose Deal

In sum, says Deborah James, director of international programs for the Washington, D.C.–based Center for Economic and Policy Research, this was a lose-lose deal for developing countries. "The tariff cuts demanded of developing countries would have caused massive job loss, and countries would have lost the ability to protect farmers from dumping, further impoverishing millions on the verge of survival," she says.

By the way, it's not as if this is a North vs. South, rich country vs. poor country issue. Although there have been multiple lines of fragmentation in the Doha negotiations, the best way to understand what's going on is that the rich country governments are driving the agenda to advance corporate interests, not those of their populations. That's why there is so little public support for the Doha trade agenda, in both rich and poor countries.

Says Lori Wallach of Public Citizen's Global Trade Watch: "Now that WTO expansion has been again rejected at this 'make or break' meeting, elected officials and those on the campaign trail in nations around the world—including U.S. presidential candidates—will be asked what they intend to do to replace the failed WTO model and its version of corporate globalization with something that benefits the majority of people worldwide."

> "Soarҳng imports during the WTO de-
> cade have contributed to the loss of
> nearly one in six U.S. manufacturing
> jobs."

The WTO Hurts the U.S. Manufacturing Industry

Lori Wallach

*Lori Wallach is the director of Public Citizen's Global Watch Di-
vision. In the following testimony before the Subcommittee on
Trade of the House Committee on Ways and Means, she outlines
the damage WTO trade agreements have wrought on the U.S.
manufacturing industry, contending that every major prediction
on the benefits free trade agreements would bring to U.S. industry was wrong.*

As you read, consider the following questions:

1. According to the author, what has been the growth in
   U.S. median income?

2. How does the author characterize the type and quality
   of jobs available during the WTO decade?

Lori Wallach, "Statement of Lori Wallach," Statement Before the Subcommittee on Trade of theCommittee on Ways and Means, House of Representatives, May 17, 2005. Reproduced by permission of the author.

3. What types of jobs are being exported overseas in recent years, according to Wallach?

On the basis of the ten-year record of the WTO in operation, Public Citizen urges Congress to demand a transformation of the current global "trade" rules which have not only failed to achieved the economic gains we were promised when Congress debated the establishment of the WTO in 1994, but have resulted in unacceptable reversals in an array of non-trade, non-economic policies and goals which promote the public interest in the United States and abroad. While this hearing is focused on the WTO's record, I urge the committee to hold a future hearing about ideas for transforming the current system to one that is more economically and environmentally sustainable and democratically accountable. Unfortunately the [George W.] Bush Administration's March annual trade report to Congress, which was also to be understood as fulfilling its statutorily required five-year report on the WTO, did not satisfy the statutory language by answering the specific questions set forth there which were designed to measure both the positive and negative results of the WTO on the United States. Rather, the March 1 report only touted the Administration's view of the WTO's benefits for the United States.

We have spent the last ten years closely monitoring and documenting the outcomes of numerous trade agreements. Beginning in 2001, we compiled these findings for a book released in 2003, entitled *Whose Trade Organization? A Comprehensive Guide to the WTO*. This book is unique in its examination of the effect of WTO rules on economic well-being and development, agriculture and food safety, the environment, public health, and democratic policy-making. This testimony summarizes and updates the major findings of the book, but I encourage any interested member of this committee to read the entire book, and we will gladly furnish a complimentary copy to your office.

Broad Concerns

During the Uruguay Round negotiations of the General Agreement on Tariffs and Trade (GATT) which established the WTO and over a dozen new substantive agreements it would enforce, Public Citizen raised concerns about the implications of establishing such broad global rules on non-trade matters in the context of an international regime whose goal was expanding trade. While expanded trade has the ability to bring benefits to consumers, workers, and farmers, setting broad non-trade rules in a body whose aim was trade expansion, threatened to undermine an array of consumer, environmental and human rights goals, the implementation of which, sometimes limits trade, such as in food containing banned pesticides. Effectively our concern was that the WTO did not mainly cover 'trade,' but rather served to implement a much more expansive corporate globalization agenda that required countries to change their domestic policies worldwide to meet the needs and goals of the world's largest multinational business interests.

We also raised deep concerns about the WTO's threat to citizen-accountable, democratic policy-making processes—in which the people who would live with the results participate in making decisions and are able to alter policies that do not meet their needs. While some problems require a global approach—such as transboundary environmental problems or weapons proliferation—others, such as setting domestic food or product safety standards or developing policies to ensure a countries' inhabitants have access to affordable medicine or basic services such as health care, education, transportation, water or other utilities do not require global redress and moreover, setting global rules on these matters can undermine democratic policy making that reflects the needs and desires of different countries' inhabitants at different times.

Warnings Went Unheeded

We sought to alert Congress as to what a dramatic shift WTO would affect in how and where non-trade policy would be set. Yet even in this hearing, much of the focus remains on the important, but not singular, implications of the WTO on trade flows. While the GATT covered only traditional trade matters, such as tariffs and quotas, with respect only to trade in goods, the WTO included agreements setting terms on the service sector; food, environmental and product safety standards; patents and copyrights; investment policy; and even the terms by which countries could make procurement decisions regarding their domestic tax dollars. The operative term of the WTO requires that "all countries shall ensure conformity of their domestic laws, regulations and administrative procedures" to all of these broad WTO requirements. As well, the WTO's Dispute Settlement Understanding (DSU) provided for a stringent enforcement mechanism, subjecting countries who fail to conform their domestic policies to the WTO dictates to trade sanctions after a tribunal process that does not guarantee the basic due process protections afforded by U.S. law, such as open hearings, access to documents, conflict of interest rules for tribunalists, or outside appeals.

In 1990 when Public Citizen began working on the Uruguay Round, we were not particularly focused on the potential implications for poor country development or on U.S. wages, income inequality or jobs. However, over 15 years of working on the GATT and then WTO, our relationships with developing country economists and policy experts, as well as our tracking of economic trends, has expanded the scope of our focus.

Now, after a decade of tracking the WTO's actual outcomes, Public Citizen's concerns about the WTO have grown dramatically. We have worked internationally with civil society and governments to promote a transformation of the existing

"Grandpa, what was manufacturing?"

"Grandpa, what was manufacturing?" by Clive Goddard. www.cartoonstock.com.

global "trade" rules contained in the WTO and oppose the expansion of the scope of the WTO. Yet, even as the negative consequences of the current rules and the model they represent increase, the current Doha Round WTO negotiations fail to address the existing problems and instead are designed to expand the WTO's jurisdiction into yet greater non-trade matters. . . .

The WTO and the U.S. Economy

In the early 1990s, many economists argued that the opening of foreign markets for U.S. exports under WTO (and NAFTA) would create U.S. jobs and increase income for U.S. workers and farmers. When Congress was preparing to vote on WTO in 1994, the President's Council of Economic Advisers informed Congress that approval of the package would increase annual U.S. GDP [gross domestic product] by $100–200 billion over the next decade. Others claimed that the WTO's adoption would lead to a decline in the U.S. trade deficit. President [Bill] Clinton even went so far as to promise that that the average American family would gain $1,700 in income annually from the WTO's adoption, which would have meant that the U.S. real median family income would have been upwards of $65,000 in 2005, or a nearly 35 percent increase since 1995. These growth projections have been shown to be wildly off the mark.

U.S. Median Income Growth Meager: U.S. median income grew only 8 percent to $52,680 in 2003—the latest numbers available. There is little reason to think that this has improved in 2004–05, since median real wages have not grown since that time. In fact, the U.S. real median wage has scarcely risen above its 1970 level (only 9 percent), while productivity has soared 82 percent over the same period, resulting in declining or stagnant standards of living for the nearly 70 percent of the U.S. population that does not have a college degree.

Trade Deficit Soars as Imports Boom: During the WTO era, the U.S. trade deficit has risen to historic levels, and approaches six percent of national income—a figure widely agreed to be unsustainable, putting the U.S. economy at risk of lowered income growth in the future. Soaring imports during the WTO decade have contributed to the loss of nearly one in six U.S. manufacturing jobs.

U.S. Has Suffered a Good-Job Export Crisis: Another factor contributing to this job loss is the shift in investment trends. . . . WTO Trade Related Investment Rules (TRIMs) limit the ability of countries to set conditions on how foreign investors operate in other countries, making it more appealing for manufacturers to seek lower wages by relocating. Meanwhile, WTO terms guaranteed low tariff access for products made in low wage countries back into wealthy markets while forbidding rich countries from setting labor or other standards such products must meet. The type and quality of jobs available for workers in the U.S. economy has dramatically shifted during the WTO decade, with workers losing to imports or offshoring their higher wage manufacturing jobs (which often also provided health care and other benefits) and finding reemployment in lower wage jobs. Labor Department data shows that such workers lose up to 27 percent of their earnings in such shifts.

U.S. Income and Wage Inequality Have Jumped: During the WTO decade these trends have resulted in U.S. income and wage inequality increasing markedly. In 1995, the top five percent of U.S. households by income made 6.5 times what the poorest 20 percent of households made, while this gap grew by nearly 10 percent by 2003. In wages, the situation was comparable. In 1995, a male worker that ranked at the 95th percentile in wages earned 2.68 times what a worker at the 20th percentile earned. By 2003, that gap had widened nearly 8 percent. Nearly all economists agree that increased trade has partially driven this widening inequality. One study by the non-partisan Center for Economic and Policy Research found that trade liberalization has cost U.S. workers without college degrees an amount equal to 12.2% of their current wages. For a worker earning $25,000 a year, this loss would be slightly more than $3,000 per year. William Cline, at the pro-WTO Institute for International Economics, estimates that about 39 percent of the actually observed increase in wage inequality is attributable to trade trends.

Job Export Crisis Is Expanding from Manufacturing to High Tech and Services: While some commentators, such as Nike CEO Phil Knight, have famously argued that this decline in assembly-line U.S. manufacturing is a result of "Americans simply not wanting to make shoes for a living," job loss and wage stagnation is increasingly affecting workers in those sectors where the United States is understood to have a comparative advantage, such as professional services and high technology. Studies commissioned by the U.S. government have shown that as many as 48,417 U.S. jobs—including many in high-tech sectors—were offshored to other countries in the first three months of 2004 alone. This trend does not appear to be slowing down, as 3.3 million high-end service sector jobs—including physicians, computer programmers, engineers, accountants and architects—are all forecast to be outsourced overseas in the next decade. Another study by the Progressive Policy Institute, a think-tank associated with the pro-WTO faction of the Democratic Party, found that 12 million information-based U.S. jobs—54 percent paying better than the median wage—are highly susceptible to such offshoring.

This manufacturing and high-tech job loss has had direct impact on workers' ability to bargain for higher real wages. Studies commissioned by the U.S. government show that as many as 62 percent of U.S. union drives face employer threats to relocate abroad, with the factory shut-down rate following successful union certifications tripling in the years after WTO relative to the years before.

In short, few of the claims made about the U.S. economic benefits that would flow from greater trade liberalization can be shown to have been close to accurate. This, however, has not stopped another round of WTO expansion from being launched, accompanied by a new set of promises.

VIEWPOINT

| "U.S. manufacturing is in very good condition today."

The U.S. Manufacturing Industry Is Doing Well

Daniel Ikenson

Daniel Ikenson is the associate director of the Cato Institute's Center for Trade Policy Studies. In the following viewpoint, he counters the prevailing belief that the U.S. manufacturing industry is in trouble, arguing that it is more robust than ever. Ikenson notes that despite the numerous stories eulogizing the demise of U.S. manufacturing, the country remains the world's most prolific manufacturer.

As you read, consider the following questions:

1. How many U.S. manufacturing jobs have been lost between 2003 and 2006, according to the author?

2. How did Ikenson rank U.S. manufacturing output in 2006?

3. How did the author rank U.S. manufacturing revenues in 2006?

Reports of the death of U.S. manufacturing have been greatly exaggerated. Since the depth of the manufacturing recession in 2002, the sector as a whole has experienced robust and sustained output, revenue, and profit growth. The year 2006 was a record year for output, revenues, profits, profit rates, and return on investment in the manufacturing sector. And despite all the stories about the erosion of U.S. manufacturing primacy, the United States remains the world's most prolific manufacturer—producing two and a half times more output than those vaunted Chinese factories in 2006.

Yet, the rhetoric on Capitol Hill and on the presidential campaign trail about a declining manufacturing sector is reaching a fevered pitch. Policymakers point repeatedly to the loss of 3 million manufacturing jobs as evidence of impending doom, even though those acute losses occurred between 2000 and 2003, and job decline in manufacturing has leveled off to historic averages.

In the first six months of the 110th Congress, more than a dozen antagonistic or protectionist trade-related bills have been introduced, which rely on the presumed precariousness of U.S. manufacturing as justification for the legislation. Justification for those bills is predicated on the belief that manufacturing is in decline and that the failure of U.S. trade policy to address unfair competition is to blame. But those premises are wrong. The totality of evidence points to a robust manufacturing sector that has thrived on account of greater international trade.

The Manufacturing Fallacy

A certain fallacy has taken hold in Washington. Too many lawmakers are operating under a mistaken trio of assumptions: that U.S. manufacturing is on the decline, that unfair foreign competition explains that decline, and that failure to formulate a policy response to arrest and reverse that trend imperils the nation's future. The ascent of those views on

Capitol Hill is a testament to the power of exaggeration, repetition, and indignation, and is a profound disservice to the truth. Some very bad policy options, predicated on those myths, are now under consideration in Congress.

It is true that the number of workers employed in U.S. manufacturing industries declined by about three million between 2000 and 2003. It is also true that real wage growth in manufacturing has been anemic since the manufacturing recession earlier in the decade. And it is correct that the manufacturing sector's contribution to GDP [gross domestic product] has been shrinking. But those data are not evidence of a declining manufacturing sector or unfair trade competition. At most, they shed some light on a sector that is in transition. And during that transition, some phenomenal operating results have been registered.

Robust Growth

Since the nadir of the manufacturing recession in 2002, the sector as a whole has experienced robust and sustained output, revenue, and profit growth, achieving gains in all three for four straight years. Two thousand and six was a record year for output, revenues, profits, profit rates, and return on investment in the manufacturing sector. And, despite all the stories about the erosion of U.S. manufacturing primacy, the United States remains the world's most prolific manufacturer—producing two and a half times more output in 2006 than those much-celebrated Chinese factories.

Of course, manufacturing is not monolithic. It comprises a variety of industries, each facing different economic circumstances. Some industries may be doing very well, while others struggle to adapt to changing circumstances. According to the findings presented in this paper, for every two U.S. manufacturing industries that experienced increases in revenue, one experienced a decline; for every two that saw their profits increase, one saw its profits decline; for every two that experienced increases in output, one experienced falling output. Thus, roughly two-thirds of U.S. manufacturing is doing well by the most traditional metrics of economic health. What about the other third? Can their lagging health be attributed to increased foreign competition? If so, are policymakers justified in intervening to try to change the tide?

This paper seeks to present the facts about the condition of U.S. manufacturing, while dispensing with some persistent myths along the way.

Proliferating Myths

Washington is abuzz with talk of U.S. manufacturing demise. Protectionists on the op-ed pages, on the airwaves, and in Congress emphasize the decline of U.S. manufacturing at the hands of insidious foreign competition, which has been enabled (if not encouraged) by an administration that has ignored the plight of blue-collar America, while tolerating unfair foreign trade practices. Reinforcing that perspective are the opinions expressed almost nightly by television talk show hosts, who seem more intent on stoking controversy than on providing a forum for honest debate.

The thrust of those messages, which continue even after several consecutive years of recovery and strong operating performance within the manufacturing sector, is that new trade policies are needed to arrest the decline of U.S. manufacturing, which would otherwise be in excellent financial health, and a reliable engine of U.S. job growth. Averting new, playing-field-leveling trade policies in the near term, so the message goes, will further erode U.S. capacity to maintain its position of global economic preeminence. . . .

Myths Gain Traction

Long after the facts on the ground have changed significantly, that message is gaining traction with policymakers. One reason for the traction is that political action tends to lag behind economic or social circumstances. In 2007 we are five years beyond the nadir of the U.S. manufacturing recession, well into recovery and even record territory. Yet, Congress appears keen to act on behalf of the sector, as if its troubles weren't several years removed. Another reason has to do with the change in control of Congress last November [2006]. An agenda that caters to the wishes of labor—and its manufacturing industry benefactors—is more likely to resonate with the new Democratic majority.

Job Losses Are the Story

The political story of manufacturing is all about job losses. Between 2000 and 2003, the number of workers employed in the U.S. manufacturing sector declined from around 17.3 million to around 14.5 million—a drop of 2.8 million workers. But since then the rate of decline has reverted to the much more modest, decades-long manufacturing average. Between 2003 and 2006, the number of workers employed in the sector dropped to 14.2 million—a decline of only 300,000 workers. And on top of that picture of stabilizing manufacturing employment, nearly all relevant statistics point to a thriving manufacturing sector.

Yet the three million jobs lost figure has become emblematic of some presumed failure of policy. That number has been cited and repeated so frequently that it is treated with a certain solemnity, a false significance, which far exceeds its utility as a measure of the condition of U.S. manufacturing then or now. The fact that the U.S. manufacturing sector has recovered fully from its recession in 2001–02, and has even reached new heights with respect to several important indicia, has been nearly totally lost in the political debate about what must be done to save manufacturing.

In March the congressional leadership unveiled its "New Trade Policy for America," which contains several policy bullet points, including the following: "Democrats offer a trade policy that will [among other things] stand up for American workers, farmers, and businesses, *especially in the hard-hit U.S. manufacturing sector.*" Democrats advocate better enforcement of trade agreements to "ensure that countries play by the rules so that trade is a two-way street."

Don't Mess with Success

For the record, last year [2006] the "hard-hit" manufacturing sector produced more output than at any other time in history, while achieving record sales and record profits (in constant dollar terms). Likewise, U.S. manufacturing exports reached record highs. Thus, trade is already a two-way street, and policymakers should resist any measures that might impede its flow.

Lawmakers are so keen to be seen doing something for manufacturing that many appear unwilling to acknowledge the sector's tremendous recovery. Such acknowledgement could deprive them of an opportunity to report back to their constituents how hard they are working for the American family.

Testifying recently at a House Ways and Means Committee trade subcommittee hearing on the merits of the Nonmarket Economy Trade Remedy Act of 2007 (a bill to, among other things, authorize the application of countervailing duties against nonmarket economies), Rep. Peter Visclosky (D-IN) offered, "My message, simply put, is that if we are to maintain a manufacturing base in the United States, we *must* have zero tolerance for unfair and illegal trade. . . . If our companies cannot count on a level playing field, then U.S. manufacturing has no long-term future." Visclosky should also consider the growing importance of export markets to U.S. manufacturers lest he think there is nothing to lose by enacting aggressive trade legislation.

Situation in Michigan

In May [2007], Democratic members of the Michigan congressional delegation as well as the state's governor issued their "American Manufacturing Initiative," billed as a "comprehensive initiative to revitalize U.S. manufacturing." In offering his support of the initiative, Sen. Carl Levin (D-MI) opined that "the [George W.] Bush Administration has not lifted a finger to support manufacturing in America while we have lost three million manufacturing jobs on its watch." Rep. John Dingell (D-MI), another sponsor of the initiative, declared: "Manufacturers are hurting in large part due to this Administration's lax attitude toward unfair trade practices."

In fairness, Michigan's political representatives may have reason to despair about their manufacturing industries. While the rest of U.S. manufacturing has recovered, Michigan's manufacturing economy remains stagnant. Real GDP growth between 2005 and 2006 in Michigan ranked dead last among the 50 states. Meager manufacturing value-added growth contributed only 0.05 percentage points to what was a net contraction of the state's economy to the tune of −0.5 percent. Nationwide, the contribution of manufacturing was .41 percentage points to an overall GDP growth rate of 3.4 percent. Had Michigan's manufacturing sector been able to contribute as much as neighboring Indiana's manufacturing sector did to its overall economy, Michigan's economy would have actually grown—by 0.3 percent.

The strength of manufacturing outside of Michigan is strong evidence that unfair trade and the administration's allegedly lax attitude toward it are not to blame for Michigan's problems. Manufacturing's woes in that state likely have more to do with the relatively high level of labor force unionization, restrictive work rules, and state laws and regulations that deter investment and business formation there.

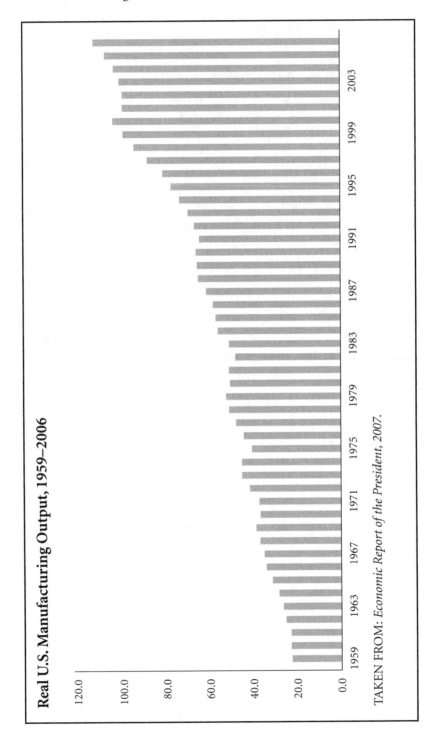

Real U.S. Manufacturing Output, 1959–2006

TAKEN FROM: *Economic Report of the President, 2007.*

Politics of Manufacturing

In the presidential debates, candidates from both major parties have spoken about our fragile manufacturing sector and the unwillingness of the current president to respond with get-tough trade policies. Responding to a question by [TV journalist] Chris Matthews about how he would be different from President Bush, Republican candidate Duncan Hunter offered: "You know, we won World War II, World War I and the Cold War with a major industrial base. We're losing our industrial base through bad trade policy right now. China is cheating on trade. I would enforce trade laws. That's something that the president is not doing."

A top priority of Democratic candidate Dennis Kucinich would be to "cancel NAFTA, cancel the WTO, go back to bilateral trade conditioned on workers' rights, [and] human rights."

Even the Democratic presidential frontrunner, Sen. Hillary Clinton, has been perpetuating the myth and spreading fear about the impact of trade on manufacturing. Voicing her opposition to the pending U.S.-South Korea Free Trade Agreement, Senator Clinton opined: "While I value the strong relationship the United States enjoys with South Korea, I believe that this agreement is inherently unfair. It will hurt the U.S. auto industry, increase our trade deficit, cost us good middle-class jobs and make America less competitive."

Issue Gets Attention

And it's not only the politicians hemming about manufacturing and trade. Informing policymakers' perspectives are trade associations and lobbying groups promoting legislation that will give them an advantage over their competition. All too often, they are aided in these efforts by print and broadcast reporters who like sensationalistic and economically divisive stories. And sometimes the testimony of pro-protection experts is no better grounded in economics than the nightly commentaries of CNN's Lou Dobbs. According to recent congressional testimony of Lawrence Mishel, an economist from the pro-union Economic Policy Institute:

> For working Americans, the effects of the enormous growth in foreign trade have been mostly negative, resulting in the loss of good-paying manufacturing jobs, significant downward pressure on wages, and increased inequality. The doubling of trade as a share of our economy over the last 25 years has been accompanied by a massive trade deficit, directly displacing several million jobs. Most of these jobs were in the manufacturing sector, which included millions of union jobs that paid better-than-average wages. In just the five years from 2000–05, more than three million manufacturing jobs disappeared. We estimate that at least one-third of that decline was caused by the rise in the manufactured goods trade deficit.

To paint this gloomy picture, Mishel ignores a host of economic facts. Since 1980 trade as a share of U.S. GDP has increased by 130 percent. Imports alone have increased six-fold. But that huge growth in trade has occurred alongside the creation of 46 million net new jobs in the United States since 1980—1.8 million net new jobs per year. Meanwhile the average U.S. unemployment rate has decreased in each successive decade: in the 1980s, it was 7.3; in the 1990s, it was 5.8; and, since 2000, it has been 5.1. As of June 2007, the unemployment rate stood at 4.5 percent.

Given the manufacturing sector's return to record sales and profitability after the phase-out of those "better-than-average" paying union jobs, the competitive burdens imposed on manufacturers by union rules and wages should be obvious.

False Premises

Despite U.S. manufacturing's overall health, in the 109th Congress more than two dozen pieces of trade legislation—most of them aimed at China—were introduced. In less than the first six months of the 110th Congress, more than one dozen pieces of trade legislation were introduced in response to, among other things, the presumed precariousness of U.S. manufacturing.

Section 1, paragraph 8 of H.R. 294, which would prohibit the United States from negotiating or entering into any new bilateral or regional trade agreements for a period of two years, reads: "United States trade policies have had a devastating impact on the manufacturing sector in the United States; an estimated 2,800,000 manufacturing jobs in the United States have been lost since 2001."

Likewise, section 1, paragraph 3 of H.R. 1002, a bill to impose import duties on Chinese goods unless and until China revalues its currency to the satisfaction of the Congress, is premised on the alleged impact of currency manipulation on U.S. manufacturing. It reads: "China's undervalued currency and the United States trade deficit with the People's Republic of China is contributing to significant United States job losses and harming United States business. In particular, the United States manufacturing sector has lost more than 3,009,000 jobs since January 2001."

Those urgent calls to arms rely on two premises: that U.S. manufacturing is in decline and that the failure of U.S. trade policy to address unfair competition is to blame. But accepting those premises requires neglect of the abundant evidence to the contrary. The totality of evidence points to a robust manufacturing sector. If that were understood by policymakers, they might be less quick to endorse provocative trade policies, particularly given that manufacturers are America's chief importers, and export markets have been manufacturing's greatest source of growth in recent years.

Real State of U.S. Manufacturing

By historic standards and relative to other countries' manufacturing sectors, U.S. manufacturing is in very good condition today. Those who speak of the demise of manufacturing often cite a few select facts: the decline in manufacturing employ-ment, that sector's diminishing contribution to gross domestic product, and the stagnation of real manufacturing wages. Those are important statistics, which should be considered in context and weighed in conjunction with other relevant data if informed conclusions are to be reached and bad policy choices avoided.

Consider the following facts. In 2006, amid record imports of manufactured products:

- Real U.S. manufacturing output reached an all-time high.

- Real manufacturing revenues reached an all-time high.

- Real manufacturing operating profits reached an all-time high.

- After-tax profit rates for manufacturing corporations reached an all-time high.

- Return on equity for manufacturing corporations reached an all-time high.

- The value of U.S. manufacturing exports reached an all-time high.

- U.S. factories remained the world's most prolific, ac-counting for over a fifth of world manufacturing value added.

Given these facts, it is extraordinarily difficult to make a serious case that our manufacturing sector has been hard hit or is in decline. Should we lament the loss of high-paying union jobs when the subsequent output and productivity sta-tistics make clear that those jobs were highly overpaid? With an overall unemployment rate of 4.5 percent and average wages outside of manufacturing surpassing average manufac-turing wages for the first time ever in 2006, it takes real creativity to paint a picture of gloom and doom. And does real manufacturing wage stagnation tell the full story of employee remuneration when firms cover a large part of their employees' dramatically increasing health care costs? Real wage growth is held back by inclusion of those inflating health care costs in the consumer price index (i.e., the denominator). Since employers cover a large part of those costs, they should be considered in the numerator as well, to ensure an apples-to-apples comparison. That's why total compensation, and not wages, is the proper metric of employee remuneration.

What about output and value added increases? How about record revenues and profits? Do they count for anything? Hasn't trade been a large net plus for the sector?

Periodical Bibliography

Leo Cendrowicz   "'We Are in the Endgame Now," *Time*, January 18, 2007.

James K. Galbraith   "What Kind of Economy?" *Nation*, February 21, 2007.

William Greider   "Born Again Rubinomics," *Nation*, July 13, 2006.

Bernard Gwertzman   "The World Is Bumpy," *Newsweek*, February 3, 2009.

Kerry Howley   "Couture Revolution," *Reason*, May 9, 2005.

Eben Kaplan and Claire Calzonetti   "The WTO's Troubled 'Doha Negotiations,'" Council on Foreign Relations, December 5, 2005.

Pascal Lamy   "Protectionism Won't Work," *Newsweek*, December 31, 2008.

Andrew Leonard   "What's So Evil About the WTO?" *Salon*, December 12, 2005. www.salon.com.

Alvaro Vargos Llosa   "The Doha Joke," *Intellectual Conservative*, May 5, 2006.

David Moberg   "Trading Down," *Nation*, December 22, 2004.

Peter Morici   "Bernanke, Chinese Currency Subsidies, and the 'P' Word," *Intellectual Conservative*, December 16, 2006.

Peter Morici   "Why Free Trade Is Failing," *Intellectual Conservative*, March 30, 2007.

Richard Nadler   "The Sovereignty Card," *American Spectator*, June 1, 2009.

Simon Robinson   "Global Trade Talks Collapse," *Time*, July 30, 2008.

OPPOSING
VIEWPOINTS®
SERIES

CHAPTER 3

How Can
The World Trade
Organization Improve?

Chapter Preface

In the early 1990s, genetically modified (GM) foods burst onto world markets, generating worldwide concern and controversy. GM foods are products grown from genetically modified organisms (GMOs), which are modified by having specific changes made to their DNA. Foods are genetically modified in order to incorporate a specific desirable trait into a organism, such as introducing a gene into soybeans to make them more resistant to certain herbicides, or adding a gene to add significant Vitamin A to rice crops.

The first commercially grown GM food was a tomato called FlavrSavr, which was modified to ripen without getting mushy. Although the FlavrSavr tomato did not engender much controversy at the time, it was ultimately beset by production problems and competition from other tomato brands and disappeared from supermarket shelves. The most common GM foods are plant products, such as soybean, corn, canola, and cottonseed oil. Animal products have been developed too. For example, a breed of pigs has been engineered to absorb plant phosphorus more efficiently, which results in a less phosphorus-filled manure.

The practice of raising GM foods has become more prevalent. As researchers, scientists, farmers, and the agriculture and food industry saw more applications for the practice, more and more GM food was developed. In 1997 GMOs were grown on 4.3 million acres of land; by 2005, GMOs were being cultivated on 222 million acres of land.

However, the exploding prevalence of GM food raised major concerns from a number of areas. One of the controversies involves the effects pest- and herbicide-resistant crops will have on ecosystems. Although crops free from herbicides or pesticides seems like a worthy goal, there are consequences to impacting the biodiversity of farmland which must be taken into account.

Another area of controversy is the safety of GM foods. Although there have not been adverse health effects caused by GM foods to date, scientists contend they do not have enough data to conclude that GM foods are safe and do not pose health risks. Many scientists argue that more testing is called for before GM food are put on the market. In certain regions of the world, concern over the safety of GM foods caused governments to take action.

In 1999 the European Union (EU) imposed a moratorium on approving new GM products as a result of mounting public concern about the safety of GM food. In fact, one EU survey showed that more than 70 percent of Europeans were opposed to GM foods. The moratorium generated opposition by many countries that produced GM foods. The United States, the world's biggest producer of GM foods, took the lead in pressuring the World Trade Organization (WTO) to force the EU into overturning the ban. In 2004 the EU agreed to lift the ban, contingent on rigorous labeling rules that ensured that consumers were informed that these products were genetically modified.

The debate over GM food and the WTO's role in the EU controversy is one of the topics covered in the following chapter. Other viewpoints explore how the WTO can impact the environment, help establish global food security, and protect intellectual property rights.

> "Increased international trade, the rules
> of the multilateral trade regime, and
> the incentives they present could be
> harnessed to support environmental ob-
> jectives."

The WTO Can Help the Environment

Margaret Lay

*Margaret Lay is a research assistant at the Federal Reserve Board
of Governors. In the following viewpoint, she elucidates the concerns about utilizing trade policy to affect environmental policy,
but then outlines the many potential positive environmental outcomes that can come from trade negotiations and policy.*

As you read, consider the following questions:

1. What is an example of a trade-distorting practice that
   the WTO and trade policy can eliminate, in Lay's opinion?

2. According to the author, what incentive convinced Russia to ratify the Kyoto Protocol?

3. What does the Stockholm Convention on Persistent Organic Pollutants prohibit, according to Lay?

Margaret Lay, "Can Trade Policy Support the Next Global Climate Agreement?" Carnegie Endowment for International Peace, September 2008. Reproduced by permission.

Can trade policy be designed to support environmental objectives? Would restricting trade on the basis of environmental concerns undermine fundamental principles of the international trade regime? Does trade increase carbon emissions or cause other types of environmental damage? Do the benefits from increased trade outweigh its possible harmful effects on the environment? These are some of the questions that color the conversation between the global trade and environment communities. . . .

From the standpoint of environmental advocates, international trade policy could both threaten the environment and create important incentives to protect it. It is useful to examine separately the concerns of the environmental community and the potential synergies between environmental objectives and the multilateral trade regime.

The Concerns

Trade liberalization has several potential negative effects on the environment. A primary objective of the global trade regime is to increase the volume of global production. This, in turn, may lead to an increased exploitation of natural resources and higher levels of carbon emissions in the production process. Transporting more goods longer distances will also result in the use of more fossil fuels. Conversely, foreign investment and competition may introduce cleaner production methods to developing countries, and the rules of the international trade regime may require countries to abandon their protection of carbon-intensive industries. The phenomenon of comparative advantage may concentrate certain production in areas where the environmental cost is relatively lower. The evidence is inconclusive on whether open borders increase or decrease global carbon emissions, hurt or help the environment.

Some environmental advocates worry about a "race to the bottom" of environmental standards: Nations that want to attract investment in carbon-intensive industry will lower national environmental standards to lower production costs; firms will escape the high costs of abiding by stringent environmental policies by moving production to these pollution havens and then exporting the goods produced to countries with higher standards; and industries in countries with high standards will suffer a loss or lobby for lower standards. Thus, a structure of comparative advantage that fails to account for the environmental cost of carbon emissions will enable the carbon emitted in the production of goods to leak from countries with high standards to those with low standards.

Environmental Standards Differ

The differential in environmental standards among countries that trade with each other also leads to emissions leakage through consumption. National climate policies target production-based, rather than consumption-based, emissions. Countries with aggressive national climate policies impose limits on the level of carbon emissions emitted by domestic producers but not on the level of carbon emitted to serve domestic consumers. Consumers in countries with strict carbon policy will often buy carbon-intensive goods imported from developing countries—the production of which resulted in higher levels of carbon emission than would have occurred had the good been produced under stricter domestic carbon policy—because those imported goods are cheaper. When they cannot control the carbon content of imports, national climate policy makers in nations participating in global trade have difficulty limiting the size of their country's carbon footprint including consumption.

Efforts to measure the level of carbon traded across borders increasingly focus on the carbon "embodied" in international trade. The embodied carbon of a good is the amount of carbon emitted throughout its lifecycle—in its production, transportation, and consumption. A new study finds that international trade embodies approximately 20 percent of global carbon dioxide emissions. This number is increasing. Another study concludes that Norway—a signatory to the Kyoto Protocol, with its carbon dioxide production emissions stabilized at 55 to 57 metric tonnes a year—increased the size of its carbon footprint including consumption by 33 percent from 2001 to 2006. Open borders can undermine national climate policy because they allow countries with stringent environmental standards to outsource their carbon emissions.

Potential Synergies

Even in the face of these concerns, increased international trade, the rules of the multilateral trade regime, and the incentives they present could be harnessed to support environmental objectives. Another primary objective of the multilateral trade regime is to eliminate trade-distorting practices. Many such practices may also be harmful to the environment; for example, subsidies to the fishing sector may encourage unsustainable fishing practices, agricultural subsidies can support environmentally harmful agricultural production, and tariffs on environmental goods and services can restrict the dissemination of clean technology. The rules of the multilateral trade regime are designed to facilitate the breaking down of these trade-distorting practices. Here, the objectives of the multilateral trade regime may lead to policies that also benefit the environment.

Further, global and national environmental policies could exploit the incentive structure created by countries' desire to access international markets. Increased market access can translate into increased demand for a nation's products and enable it to expand production, income, and welfare. The last half century of the expansion of international trade and the multilateral trade regime, and the concurrent growth in many developing countries, has demonstrated the power of this incentive. Nations have dramatically shifted their national economic and trade policies so that they could be accepted into the WTO and reap the benefits of expanded trade. These same incentives can be harnessed to shape national climate and environmental policies and commitments.

Incentives and Threats Work

Trade incentives and trade threats have convinced countries to join multilateral environmental agreements (MEAs). Russia, for example, agreed to ratify the Kyoto Protocol in exchange for EU support for its bid to join the WTO in 2004. The Montreal Protocol employed a multilateral trade threat to encourage developing countries to sign it in 1987. The proposed EU carbon tariff is an example of a unilateral trade threat that could convince the United States and China to cooperate with global climate initiatives—but the success of this threat remains to be seen.

Trade incentives and tools can affect the behavior of firms as well as the climate policy of particular nations. Trade restrictions on environmentally harmful products could encourage firms to reduce their production of those products by shrinking the international market. The Stockholm Convention on Persistent Organic Pollutants, for example, prohibits member countries from importing banned substances unless the import is from another member country and destined for environmentally sound disposal. The aim is to reduce the amount of persistent organic pollutants that firms in both member and nonmember countries supply by systematically reducing the demand for those pollutants.

Create a Market

Trade mechanisms could also appeal to a global firm's need to improve efficiency by enforcing high environmental standards in key markets. Suppose a critical threshold of countries were to enact trade restrictions according to a unified system of stringent environmental standards. If the market that these countries constitute is large enough, global firms will do what is necessary to compete in it. These firms—even if they are making their products in nations that do not adhere to the system of stringent standards—would have to abide by these standards to sell in this threshold market. Moreover, it is often inefficient for such firms to produce multiple lines of products, intended for distinct markets, that adhere to different environmental standards. Thus, to improve microefficiency, these firms may adopt the stringent environmental standards for all production.

A shift in the behavior of global firms in developing countries could even encourage a change in national environmental standards, just as high energy-efficiency standards in California led to the improvement of these standards throughout the United States. California, the first state to adopt efficiency standards for appliances in 1977, set efficiency standards equivalent to the efficiency of high-performing appliances already on the market and upgraded them throughout the 1980s. As more states followed California's lead, national appliance manufacturers, inconvenienced by diverse efficiency standards across states, joined with efficiency advocates to lobby for a uniform national standard. Thus California's ambitious standards guided the development of a similar national standard. On the international market, firms face different efficiency standards in different countries. Many MEAs seek to harmonize international standards. The enforcement of high national standards through trade restrictions could act as a similar guiding force on the international stage of efficiency standards, and likewise could provide the impetus for including emissions standards in a multilateral climate agreement.

"Under the proposed WTO rules on Services, governments could be required to let foreign corporations violate environmental standards."

The WTO Hurts the Environment

Deborah James

Deborah James is the director of International Programs of the Center for Economic and Policy Research. In the following viewpoint, she argues that free trade agreements like the North American Free Trade Agreement (NAFTA) and Central American Free Trade Agreement (CAFTA) and certain agreements of the World Trade Organization will threaten global biodiversity, facilitate the spread of genetically modified crops and the exploitation of natural resources, and accelerate global climate change.

As you read, consider the following questions:

1. Why do CAFTA and the Free Trade Area of the Americas prohibit member countries from enacting many new environmental regulations, in James's opinion?

2. What does the author define as "bioprospecting"?

Deborah James, "Free Trade and the Environment," *Global Exchange*, October 28, 2007. Reproduced by permission.

3. According to James, what are the dangers of the WTO agreement on Non-Agricultural Market Access (NAMA)?

For decades, governments have worked together through the United Nations to develop agreements to protect the natural resources of our shared planet. Unfortunately, so-called "free trade agreements" threaten to erode many of the advances in global environmental protection, endangering our planet and the natural resources necessary to support life. The North American Free Trade Agreement (NAFTA) and certain agreements of the World Trade Organization (WTO) were written to prioritize rights for corporations over protections for our shared environment.

But rather than being repealed, corporate interests are negotiating the expansion of these corporate rights. The U.S.-Dominican Republic-Central American Free Trade Agreement (CAFTA), . . . and the proposed Free Trade Area of the Americas (FTAA), . . . are modeled on NAFTA. In addition, negotiations are proceeding within the WTO to expand many of its policies.

These new agreements threaten global biodiversity, would accelerate the spread of genetically engineered (GE) crops, increase natural resource exploitation, further degrade some of the most critical environmental regions on the planet, and erode the public's ability to protect our planet for future generations.

No Environmental Protections

Neither CAFTA nor the FTAA require member countries to adopt internationally recognized standards for environmental protection. Nor does either agreement ensure that member countries don't lower or waive their existing environmental laws in an effort to attract investment. What's more, rules in CAFTA and the FTAA would actually prohibit member countries from enacting many new environmental regulations, allowing those regulations to be challenged as "barriers to trade." This strips the public from a fundamental democratic right to pass laws that protect our environment in favor of corporations' "right" to profit from environmental destruction.

Megadiverse Countries

Latin America is one of the most biologically and culturally diverse regions on the planet. Four of the five Central American countries included in CAFTA have tropical areas that have been identified as "critical regions" for their biodiversity. Additionally, 7 of the world's 12 "megadiverse" countries (Mexico, Brazil, Venezuela, Peru, Ecuador, Costa Rica and Colombia) are found in the Americas. "Megadiversity" countries represent the majority of the world's biodiversity and surviving Indigenous peoples, the true guardians of biodiversity. Unfortunately, so-called "free trade" agreements directly contradict important international legislation designed to protect the rights of Indigenous peoples and biodiversity, like the Convention on Biological Diversity as well as the International Labor Organization Convention 169, which states that Indigenous groups must be consulted on issues that affect their rights to land and livelihood.

Piracy of Global Biodiversity

In the last decade, the biodiversity of the Americas has been targeted by "life science" corporations (the growing consolidation of pharmaceutical, agrichemical and seed companies) in search of "green gold." These corporations are pillaging humankind's patrimony of traditional knowledge and biodiversity to create and patent drugs and agricultural products to sell for profit. The quest to patent life forms, especially medicinal plants and crops, threatens our food security, access to health care, and the biological and cultural diversity of the Americas.

Intellectual property rules in CAFTA and the FTAA would require that member countries grant protections to the patenting of life forms. This would facilitate a massive increase in "bioprospecting" or the practice of corporations patenting Indigenous communities' knowledge of plants and then profiting from that knowledge—while forcing Indigenous communities to pay for what they had previously held in common.

No GE Food Labeling

Despite the fact that independent polls in virtually every country on the planet demonstrate that people want genetically-engineered (GE) foods labeled, corporations and the U.S. government have refused to do so. Giant agribusiness multinationals ADM and Cargill have generally refused to segregate GE from non-GE crops, eliminating consumer choice and imposing GE foods on consumers. With CAFTA and the FTAA, labeling laws would be prohibited as "more burdensome than necessary" for agribusiness investors.

More GE Contamination

Dozens of crops have been developed and domesticated in the Americas over the last 10,000 years, including corn and potatoes, two of the world's most important crops for food security. The traditional cradles of food diversity are threatened by encroaching genetic contamination. The experience of Mexico under NAFTA offers an example of what's to come for Central America under CAFTA. NAFTA forced open protected Mexican corn markets to a flood of cheap imports of corn from the U.S. Corn imports into Mexico have displaced at least one and a half million farmers and are steadily eroding the genetic diversity of thousands of native corn varieties. Then, in September 2001, genetic contamination of native corn varieties was discovered as a result of the introduction of artificially low-priced GE corn from the United States under NAFTA. The expansion of GE crops threatens food security around the world.

Dolphin Laws Undermined

After years of sustained trade law challenges, the [George W.] Bush administration decided to quietly implement a change to a "dolphin safe" labeling policy which Mexico had demanded as necessary to implement a GATT ruling. (Mexico had threatened a new WTO case if their demands were not met.) On New Year's Eve 2002, when few Americans were focused on policy matters, the Bush administration announced that it would change the "Flipper-friendly" tuna policy to allow the "dolphin-safe" label to be used on tuna caught using deadly purse seine nets and dolphin encirclement.

Public Citizen, Global Trade Watch, 2009.

CAFTA and the FTAA completely disregard international law, such as the Cartagena Protocol on Biosafety, designed to regulate the cultivation and trade of genetically modified organisms.

Bill of Rights for Corporations?

While limiting public regulation for environmental protections, CAFTA and the FTAA would grant expansive powers to corporations. CAFTA's investor protections are modeled after one of the most hotly contested sections in NAFTA—its Chapter 11—a virtual Bill of Rights for corporations. These provisions allow corporations to sue governments for "damages" if a government law affects their profits. Chapter 11 of NAFTA has undermined the sovereignty of democratically elected governments, and their ability to act in the public interest. An issue over a Quebec environmental law banning specific pesticides reveals how these provisions undermine environmental protection.

Quebec law bans a popular weed killer called 2,4-D, which is considered a possible human carcinogen, and has been shown to adversely affect the immune system and reproductive functions in humans, among other impacts.

But now a corporate lobbying group representing some of the makers of the pesticide are threatening to challenge the law by suing the Canadian government under NAFTA's Chapter 11. The provincial government of Quebec and Canadian taxpayers have been given a harsh choice: pay the corporations millions of dollars in future lost profits, or repeal the law. Similar Chapter 11 cases have led to the overturn of environmental laws and millions of dollars in fines paid to corporations. If CAFTA is enacted, investor-to-state lawsuits will be spread to the corporations of six additional countries, threatening critical environmental protection in the U.S. and Central America.

Limiting Public Regulations

Both CAFTA and an agreement currently under negotiation in the WTO covering Services would make it increasingly difficult for governments to regulate and limit multinational corporate activity in environmentally-damaging activities such as oil extraction, forestry, electricity generation, road construction, and waste incineration in the interests of environmental protection.

In addition, under the proposed WTO rules on Services, governments could be required to let foreign corporations violate environmental standards. For instance, requirements that a percentage of electricity be produced from environmentally-friendly energy sources could be found to "discriminate" against foreign service companies if those companies don't provide environmentally-friendly energy, and would have to be scrapped under proposed WTO rules—even if the standard is the most effective way to protect the environment.

Natural Resources and the WTO

Corporate interests are also negotiating the expansion of the WTO through an agreement on Non-Agricultural Market Access, or NAMA. Primarily involving industrial manufactured goods, NAMA also includes trade in natural resources such as forest products, gems and minerals, and fishing and fish products. NAMA aims to reduce tariffs as well as decreasing or eliminating so-called Non-Tariff Barriers (NTBs), which can include measures for environmental protection and community development.

Eliminating tariffs in natural resources would dramatically increase their exploitation. The World Forum of Fish-harvesters and Fish-workers has warned of the devastation to fish conservation posed by NAMA. Even the U.S. Trade Representative has acknowledged that eliminating tariffs on wood products would dramatically increase logging, exacerbating deforestation in some of the world's most sensitive forests.

The WTO has already identified a wide range of environmental policy tools as potential 'barriers to trade': the certification of sustainably-harvested wood and fish products; restrictions on trade in harmful chemicals; and packaging, marketing and labeling requirements such as organic and Fair Trade labeling.

Increased Trade Increases Oil Dependency

Increasing trade increases our consumption of and dependency on oil, which has created a massive global crisis of human-induced climate change. The rise of global temperatures means more severe droughts and floods that will literally change the face of the Earth; the loss of coastal lands and the destruction of forests; an increase in heat waves and other human health hazards; and the extinction of plant and animal species. Our consumption of oil also leads to violations of the human rights of peoples in oil-producing countries such as Ecuador, Colombia, Indonesia, and Nigeria, who suffer environmental heath problems, displacement, and contamination of their communities. Increased trade—and hence dependence on oil—will also contribute to global insecurity by providing further incentive for the drive towards war as the U.S. government straggles for control over this most strategic global resource.

Environmentalists Oppose CAFTA

Most environmental organizations in the United States have written letters to the U.S. Trade Representative and members of the U.S. Congress, voicing their opposition to CAFTA. Groups as diverse as Center for International Environmental Law, Defenders of Wildlife, Earthjustice, Friends of the Earth, League of Conservation Voters, National Environmental Trust, Natural Resources Defense Council, National Wildlife Federation, the Sierra Club, and U.S. PIRG have sounded out a warning about CAFTA's negative potential impact on our shared environment. And in Central America, over 800 social organizations—including many environmental groups—signed a petition in July of 2004 urging the U.S. Congress to reject CAFTA.

Stop CAFTA and WTO Expansion

"Free trade" agreements are generally little more than code words for corporate expansion across the globe at the expense of communities and our environment.... But we can ... work for global trade agreements that protect our planet for generations to come.

> "The [WTO's] TRIPS Agreement re-
> quires that all WTO members recog-
> nize patents on products like pharma-
> ceuticals and genetically enhanced
> crops."

The WTO Must Defend Biotechnological Intellectual Property Rights

Ronald Bailey

Ronald Bailey is a columnist for Reason *magazine and Reason
.com, where he writes a weekly science and technology column.
In the following viewpoint, he asserts that strong intellectual
property rights agreements are needed to protect the inventors,
who spend much time, effort, and money to develop products—
like lifesaving medicines—that will benefit all segments of society.*

As you read, consider the following questions:

1. How long do patents usually last, according to the author?

2. How does Bailey describe the WTO's TRIPS agreement?

3. According to the author, what is the compromise negotiators reached before the Cancun meeting on medicines in third-world countries?

"No Patents on Life," is one of the most frequently heard slogans among anti-globalization activists at the World Trade Organization's 5th Ministerial meeting. It is part of a fierce fight over intellectual property rights. Who has the right to make pharmaceuticals and who has the right to grow genetically enhanced crop plants are hotly in dispute at the WTO conference.

"Patenting of life forms must be prohibited in order to preserve biodiversity, food security and indigenous peoples' rights and protect them from corporate grip on genetic resources," declared a group of Green and Socialist parliamentarians at a press conference [during the WTO conference]. Andrew Kimbrell, director of the US-based International Center for Technology Assessment, denounced biotechnology patents as "biocolonialism" and just a continuation of the "brutal history of oppression of colonialism."

But biotechnology patents are not the only intellectual property rights fight going on at the WTO. Tony Clarke, from the Canadian anti-free trade Polaris Institute, declared at the "teach-in" run by the International Forum on Globalization (IFG), "Essential medicines should be available to the people!" Indian public health activist Mira Shiva asked, "Why should the poor suffer and die if lifesaving medicines are available?"

A Short Lesson on Rights

But, before considering the objections being raised by anti-globalization activists to intellectual property rights, a short lesson in intellectual property rights: Property rights over things like land, houses and cars are easily understood by everyone. Fences protect land and locks protect houses and cars from being stolen or misused by others. But intellectual property by its nature cannot be protected by fences and locks. For example, once an inventor has devised, say, a recipe for a powerful new drug, another drug manufacturer who finds out that recipe can easily make it. That means that the inventor, who spent the time, effort and money, to bring the benefit of a new cure to humanity would not be compensated for his labor. Patents are designed to remedy that situation by providing strong incentives to inventors of beneficial products.

Patents are temporary monopolies, usually 20 years in duration, which aim to achieve two things. First, in order to receive a patent, an inventor must disclose how to make the product, so that someone else can do it once the patent has expired. Second, by awarding a temporary monopoly to inventors, intellectual property rights encourage inventors to seek new discoveries by allowing them to make money either by licensing their patents to others who must pay them or by giving them the exclusive right to make the product without competition for 20 years. Abraham Lincoln once described patents as "adding the fuel of interest to the fire of genius." Simply glancing up, we can all easily see how much we have benefited by this system of encouraging inventors; nearly every product that we use in everyday life was once patented.

The TRIPS Agreement

Under the WTO, intellectual property rights, including patents, fall under an agreement called the "Trade Related Aspects of Intellectual Property Rights"(TRIPS). The TRIPS Agreement requires that all WTO members recognize patents on products like pharmaceuticals and genetically enhanced crops. Without worldwide patent protection, a company in South Africa could manufacture a product based on a Brazilian patent and then ship the product back to Brazil, undercutting the Brazilian patentholder. Perhaps in the short run Brazilian consumers might be slightly better off because they could buy the cheaper South African version of the product, but in the long run they (and we) would be worse off because future inventors would have less incentive to make new inventions and to disclose their methods to the rest of us.

But what about the poor in places like Africa, Latin America and India, who are being ravaged by diseases like AIDS? After all, it only costs a few cents to make an anti-viral pill since the formula for it was devised several years ago by big drug companies in the United States and Europe. Again, the research costs to find and develop drugs that can successfully treat AIDS were in the hundreds of millions of dollars, yet once the right formulation is discovered, it costs only a few cents to produce each actual pill. Think of it this way: the first pill cost $500 million to make, the second pill cost 5 cents. Yet selling the second, third, and thousands more pills at 5 cents each will not recover the money spent on the research necessary to make the first pill.

If researchers can't recover their costs, they will stop doing research and we will all be worse off as the pipeline for powerful new medicines goes dry. During the last half century the vast majority of new drugs which have greatly improved the health of millions in both the developed and developing countries were produced by for-profit pharmaceutical companies. Without the discoveries of pharmaceutical companies, scores of millions of people across the world would have died before their time or lived diminished lives wracked with painful and crippling diseases.

In Search of a Compromise

Nevertheless, it is a tragedy that hundreds of millions of poor people in the developing world cannot afford modern treatments. How can their needs for medicines be met without destroying the system of intellectual property rights that has made miracle medicines possible in the first place?

WTO negotiators reached a compromise just before coming to Cancun which allows poor countries to import inexpensive generic versions of medicines that are still under patent in the developed world. It is not a perfect solution—it will require extra policing to make sure that genetic versions don't undercut the patented versions being sold in developed countries. And even more problematically, this compromise will probably discourage pharmaceutical companies from investing in future research on diseases that disproportionately afflict poor people in the developing world. Why? Because the companies know that whatever they develop will be copied and sold cheaply before they can recoup their costs. So the poor may benefit from this compromise in the short run, but suffer in the long run as the development of new and better drugs aimed at diseases in the developing world slows. To answer Shiva's question: More of the poor may suffer and die because new and better drugs will not be available in the future.

Debate over Biotechnology Patents

Biotechnology patents, especially patents relating to crop biotechnology, also are under attack by anti-globalization activists. First, many experts acknowledge that many biotechnology patents are far too broad and vague and that the biotechnology patent system desperately needs refinement. However, that does not mean that the concept of biotechnology patents is wrong. Like any other area of research and discovery, biotechnology patents play a vital role in encouraging the development of superior new products.

Of course, genetically enhanced crops are one of the more contentious issues in world trade now because of the dispute between the United States and the European Union over the safety of foods made from them. Without revisiting that topic, suffice it to say that of the hundreds of millions of people who have eaten foods made from currently available biotech crops, there has not been a single documented case of a person who has suffered so much as a sniffle or a bellyache after consuming them.

The Issue of Biopiracy

"Biopiracy" is what particularly upsets activists like Andrew Kimbrell. He and other anti-globalization activists accuse transnational corporations like Monsanto and Syngenta of stealing genes nurtured by poor farmers of the world. The greedy corporations allegedly do this by patenting valuable genes found in local varieties of plants grown by traditional farmers. Then the companies try to sell the patented genes back to the poor farmers from which they took them. Sounds pretty unscrupulous, doesn't it?

What actually happens is that researchers at companies like Monsanto and Bayer screen a wide variety of plants seeking genes for things like disease resistance or particular nutrients. Say, hypothetically that the researchers find a gene in a local variety of rice in India that prevents a fungal disease endemic to India. Delighted, the corporate researchers have the technology to put the anti-fungus gene into a high yielding, but fungus prone, wheat variety. Farmers in India would have liked to grow the high yield wheat, but didn't do so because of its susceptibility to fungus.

Genes are resources the same way that something like, say, copper is a resource. If I had a rock containing copper ore, which is not much of a resource to me, perhaps I could use it as a paperweight. However, a copper rock is a much more valuable resource to someone who has the skill to mine, mill, refine, design, and market copper products, electrical wires, pots, and computer chips. Surely, it would be unreasonable for me to demand of the person who buys my copper rock and turns it into a pot that he give me the pot for free. The same goes for a beneficial gene, like the hypothetical anti-fungus gene that is inaccessible to Indian farmers because they have no way to get it from rice into wheat where it would be really helpful to them. Thanks to biotechnology, Indian farmers can now choose to grow (or not grow) the high yield wheat without fear that their crop will be devastated by fungus. BioPiracy is as much a fiction as CopperPiracy.

The anti-globalization activists get it almost exactly backward. Intellectual property rights, far from being harmful to the poor, are in fact the foundation upon which many technologies that will help them rise from poverty to prosperity will be built.

> *"Even when the consequences are literally life or death, companies are eager to utilize the World Trade Organization for their limitless hunger for profits."*

The WTO's Biotechnology Patent Rules Threaten Millions of Lives

Amitabh Pal

Amitabh Pal is the managing editor of the Progressive. *In the following viewpoint, Pal contends that Western corporations use trade agreements and institutions such as the World Trade Organization to negate local laws and make record profits. Pal concludes that these corporations value profits over the lives of millions of people.*

As you read, consider the following questions:

1. How many pending patent applications does the author say are waiting to be reviewed in India under the new law?

Amitabh Pal, "Corporate Globalization Kills," *The Progressive*, February 16, 2007. Reproduced by permission of The Progressive, 409 East Main Street, Madison, WI 53703, www.progressive.org.

2. What will be the effect if Gilead Sciences successfully receives its patent for its antiretroviral drug Viread in India, according to Pal?

3. What led to India becoming the "pharmacy of the world's poor," in the author's opinion?

Globalization is a battering ram for Western corporations. And even when the consequences are literally life or death, companies are eager to utilize the World Trade Organization for their limitless hunger for profits.

India Court Case

Take a pending court case in India. It has the potential to adversely affect the health of not only the more than 1 billion Indian citizens but of patients throughout the developing world.

In 2005, India's parliament amended its patent laws to comply with WTO rules, in spite of warnings by health experts that this would result in affordable medicines being no longer available in the country. "Amit Sen Gupta, head of the Delhi Science Forum, a scientists' group, worries that product patents will turn the clock back to the 1960s, when Western drug companies dominated India, set high prices and conducted little research on tropical diseases that, like leprosy and malaria, do not affect Americans or Europeans," the *New York Times* reported.

I was traveling by train in India a few months after the 2005 law was passed and entered into a conversation with a person who owned and operated a small pharmaceutical firm. When I asked him about the possible effects of the new patent law, he responded that it was too soon to assess the impact but that the long-term effects could be disastrous for Indian drug manufacturers.

Well, all these fears seem to be proving correct now. A significant court challenge has been launched in Indian courts by the Swiss pharmaceutical behemoth Novartis to stake its proprietary right over a leukemia drug.

Western Firms File Court Challenges

And Novartis is far from the only Western pharmaceutical firm to have sought to assert a patent claim in India. In fact, the BBC reports that 9,000 pending patent applications are waiting to be reviewed in India under the new law! In another significant court case, the U.S.-based Gilead Sciences has attempted to press its claim for a patent for its antiretroviral drug Viread in India, a move that would make cheaper Indian versions unavailable in a host of nations.

"These generic drugs are not only consumed in India," Leena Menghaney of the Nobel-winning Doctors Without Borders told the *New York Times*. "People in Africa and the Caribbean are relying on India to produce these drugs. . . . The quality matches that of U.S.-manufactured drugs, but the prices are affordable."

To give an example of the burden that will be imposed on poor patients in the developing world if the strategy of Western pharmaceutical firms succeeds, Gilead's Viread costs nearly $6,000 per patient per year in the West. A generic version of the drug made by an Indian pharmaceutical, Cipla, costs $700, with the chair of the company, Yusuf Hamied, promising that it would be made available in Africa for half that cost. But all this could be imperiled if companies like Gilead have their way in Indian courts. Realizing the potentially life-threatening consequences of this issue, AIDS activists in India are waging a number of campaigns involving such drugs, including against Gilead and the British giant GlaxoSmithKline.

Earlier Laws Pave the Way

A bit of background: In 1970, India under the Indira Gandhi government amended its patent law to have patents awarded only for processes to make medicines, not for the final prod-

Universal Access to AIDS Treatment: Targets and Challenges

Region (lower- and middle-income countries)	Antiretroviral therapy coverage	Estimated number of people receiving antiretroviral therapy	Estimated number of people needing antiretroviral therapy
Sub-Saharan Africa	30%	2,120,000	7,000,000
Eastern and southern Africa	32%	1,690,000	5,300,000
West and central Africa	25%	430,000	1,700,000
Latin America and the Caribbean	62%	390,000	630,000
Latin America	64%	360,000	560,000
The Caribbean	43%	30,000	70,000
East, South and South-East Asia	25%	420,000	1,700,000
Europe and Central Asia	17%	54,000	320,000
North Africa and the Middle East	7%	7,000	100,000
Total	31%	2,990,000	9,700,000

TAKEN FROM: avert.org, 2009.

ucts. This enabled Indian pharmaceutical firms to alter the processes slightly and make cheaper versions of essentially the same products sold by Western firms in India for astronomical prices. The result?

"India became the 'pharmacy of the world's poor' in 1970 when it stopped issuing patents for medicines," the BBC states. "This allowed its many drug producers to create generic copies of medicines still patent-protected in other countries—at a fraction of the price charged by Western drug firms."

Law Changes Lives

The changed law also dramatically improved lives in India. "At the time, India's drug prices were among the highest in the world," wrote the *New York Times* a few years ago. "Now they are among the lowest. Access to drugs is one reason that average life expectancy has risen to 64 today."

Now all of this is being jeopardized, with grave health consequences. The BBC quotes Doctors Without Borders as saying that a number of Indian firms have already stopped producing some generic AIDS drugs because of the possible legal ramifications.

Greed knows no limit for some corporations. Even when it involves the lives of millions.

> *"The less developed nations of Asia, Africa, and Latin America ... will continue to be shut out of the important European market by [EU] policymakers' callous, pernicious obstructionism."*

The WTO Should Force the EU to End Its Moratorium on Genetically Modified Food

Gregory Conko

Gregory Conko is a senior fellow at the Competitive Enterprise Institute. In the following viewpoint, he argues that the European Union moratorium on genetically modified (GM) food is illegal and without scientific merit. Conko concludes that the EU needs a more enlightened policy that acknowledges the scientific superiority of GM food and needs to follow World Trade Organization policy on the issue.

As you read, consider the following questions:

1. When was the original WTO deadline on the cessation of the EU moratorium on GM food, according to the author?

Gregory Conko, "Europe's Continued Hostility to GM Crops Runs Afoul of Science, WTO," *Competitive Enterprise Institute*, January 23, 2007. Reproduced by permission.

2. What did French president Nicolas Sarkozy do in October 2007 regarding the EU moratorium, according to Conko?

3. What scientific institutions have endorsed the safety of GM food, according to the author?

France, Germany, and the United Kingdom may have new leaders who bring the promise overall of better trans-Atlantic relations, but when it comes to the politics of global trade, some things never change. This month [January 2008], the European Union missed yet another deadline for correcting its illegal regulation of gene-spliced, or "genetically modified" (GM), crop varieties, following a World Trade Organization decision in November 2005 that some European countries were breaking international trade rules by prohibiting the import of GM foods and crops.

Although the WTO bluntly scolded the EU for imposing a moratorium on gene-spliced crop approvals from 1998 to 2004, that finding was a foregone conclusion. European politicians, including then-EU Environment Commissioner Margot Wallström, had acknowledged that the moratorium was "an illegal, illogical, and otherwise arbitrary line in the sand."

Bans Are Blatant Violations

The WTO also made clear that national bans on certain gene-spliced foods in Austria, France, Germany, Greece, Italy, and Luxembourg were blatant violations both of those countries' treaty obligations and EU rules, but the European Commission has been impotent in persuading its rogue members to conform to EU policies. Not only are most of those national bans still in place but, in October 2007, French President Nicolas Sarkozy implemented a new moratorium on the commercial cultivation of gene-spliced corn.

The most important victory for the United States and its partners was the WTO's judgment that the European Com-

GM Food Benefits Small Farmers

As much as 40% of conventional crop productivity in Africa and Asia is lost to insect pests, weeds, and plant diseases. But many of the same GM crops available in North America are already helping poor farmers in South Africa, India, China, and the Philippines combat often-voracious insects while reducing the amount of insecticides or eliminating them altogether. Indeed, studies of South African and Chinese cotton growers suggest that small farmers actually achieve disproportionately higher benefits from GM relative to larger competitors, because expensive machinery can at times be made obsolete.

Gregory Conko and C.S. Prakesh,
Wall Street Journal, *May 13, 2003.*

mission failed to abide by its own regulations by "undue delaying" of approvals for 25 gene-spliced food products. The culprit here was (and is) the European Commission's highly politicized, sclerotic [inflexible], two-stage approval process: Each application first must be cleared for marketing by various scientific panels, and then voted on by politicians, who routinely undo the scientific decisions.

As the WTO pointed out, the relevant EC scientific committees had recommended approval of all 25 product applications. But, for transparently political reasons rather than concerns about consumer health or environmental protection, EU politicians repeatedly refused to sign off on the final approvals.

GM Foods Are Safe

It is important to recall that these are *superior* products made with state-of-the art technology that is both more precise and predictable than other techniques for the genetic improvement of plants. The safety and importance of GM technology have been endorsed by dozens of scientific bodies around the world, including the French Academies of Science and Medicine, U.K. Royal Society, U.S. National Academy of Sciences, American Medical Association, and many others.

The good news is that the WTO chastised the European Union for failing to follow its own regulatory rules. The bad news is the absence from the panel report of any condemnation of those rules themselves, in spite of the fact that they are blatantly unscientific and excessive, and are clear violations of the trade treaties enforced by the WTO. Under the various WTO-enforced treaties, member countries are free to enact any level of environmental or health regulations they choose—as long as (1) every such regulation is based on the results of a risk analysis showing that some legitimate risk exists, and (2) the degree of regulation is proportional to that risk.

Every risk analysis performed by countless scientific bodies worldwide has shown that the splicing of new genes into plants, per se, introduces no incremental risks. A 2001 European Commission report summarizing the conclusions of 81 different EU-funded research projects spanning fifteen years concluded that, because GM plants and foods are made with highly precise and predictable techniques, they are at least as safe and often safer than their conventional counterparts. In 2003, then-EU Commissioner for Health and Consumer Affairs David Byrne acknowledged that the official European Commission position was that currently marketed GM crop varieties posed no greater food safety or environmental threat than the corresponding conventional food varieties.

EU Needs Enlightened Policies

None of this has translated into more enlightened decisions on either policy or individual products, however (although over the past few years the EU has approved a small, token number of gene-spliced product applications in order to pretend that its regulatory apparatus is now in compliance with the WTO ruling). By requiring extraordinary testing procedures for an admittedly safer technology, the EU's approach is not only disproportionate but actually manifests an *inverse* relationship between the degree of risk and amount of regulatory scrutiny. This is both absurd and illegal, but at a "background" briefing in February 2006, an unnamed "EU official" noted that, "[i]t is nevertheless clear, beyond any doubt, that the EU will not have to modify its GMO legislation and authorization procedures."

Because uncertainty is anathema to R&D [research and development], few companies are likely to risk the tens of millions of dollars in regulatory costs needed to pursue new GM products in Europe. Even worse, the less developed nations of Asia, Africa, and Latin America, which once anticipated that agricultural and food biotechnology could provide them a brighter and more self-sufficient future, will continue to be shut out of the important European market by policymakers' callous, pernicious obstructionism.

| "The World Trade Organization deci-
| sion [to disallow the EU ban of GM
| food] nullifies democracy at all levels."

The WTO Should Uphold the EU Moratorium on Genetically Modified Food

David Moberg

David Moberg is a senior editor at In These Times *magazine. In the following viewpoint, he asks, if the capitalistic system respects and values the role of the consumer, why is the U.S. government looking to manipulate world markets by using the World Trade Organization to end a European Union (EU) moratorium on genetically modified (GM) food. Moberg accuses the United States of being subservient to big corporations like Monsanto and throwing aside democratic and free-market principles.*

As you read, consider the following questions:

1. When did the U.S.-EU dispute start, according to Moberg?

2. According to the author, what did the WTO rule on the issue of GM food?

David Moberg, "Consumers, Citizens Must Demand Information on Biotech Food," *The Progressive*, February 15, 2006. Reproduced by permission of The Progressive, 409 East Main Street, Madison, WI 53703, www.progressive.org.

3. In a February 2006 poll, what percentage of Europeans is worried about GM products, as reported by Moberg?

America's business and political leaders constantly argue that, in a free-market system, the consumer is king. And they also declare that democracy, where the people rule, is the best form of government.

So why is the U.S. government cheering its recent victory at the World Trade Organization in a case that tramples the sovereignty of the people as both citizens and consumers?

Summary of Dispute

The dispute started in 2003, when the United States, with support from Argentina and Canada, accused the European Union of illegally blocking sales of genetically engineered agricultural products.

In its decision, the World Trade Organization panel of judges did not say whether they thought genetically engineered crops were safe. But they did rule that the European Union system was too slow and this pace amounted to an illegal moratorium, though a few crops have recently been given the green light.

European governments and the general public have had strong doubts about the environmental and health effects of genetically engineered food products. They have had much stricter procedures for reviewing the safety of such products than in the United States, where the relatively lax and corporate-influenced review process has repeatedly been criticized as inadequate by the National Research Council, a body of scientists that advises the federal government.

As a result, the U.S. Food and Drug Administration says that developers of genetically engineered products are responsible for their products' safety. But the spokesman for Monsanto, the major corporate force behind genetically engineered

"All our produce is local . . . I'd recommend the battery chicken baked in hydrogensulphide with polymorphene," by Fran. www.cartoonstock.com.

crops, says, "Monsanto should not have to vouch for the safety of biotech food. Our interest is in selling as much of it as possible."

U.S. Strong-Arming of the EU

Individual European countries have been adamant about safeguards against genetically engineered foods. Nine countries have now enacted their own moratoriums, which European environment ministers overwhelmingly endorsed but the WTO panel judged was in violation of trade rules.

The European Union also has rules requiring that genetically engineered products be traceable and clearly labeled. The Institute for Agriculture and Trade Policy expects the United States to challenge these rules next, according to spokesman Ben Lilliston.

The primary international treaty covering these issues— the Cartagena Protocol on Biosafety that went into effect in 2003 (despite U.S. refusal to sign)—grants nations the rights to take precautions to protect consumers and the environment. That means countries can require that products are proven safe before allowing them to be sold on their soil.

Consumer Preferences Ignored

European public opinion supports taking strict precautions. A poll earlier this month [February 2006] indicated that 62 percent of all Europeans are worried about genetically engineered products, and another poll showed 78 percent of French people favor a temporary ban.

So if the consumer is king, why don't American farmers and export companies simply produce what their customers want?

The problem is that corporations like Monsanto have sold American farmers on biotech crops, the federal government wants to support some of these corporations, and the [George W.] Bush administration wants to weaken government regulation wherever it can.

The administration is also attempting to delude farmers into thinking that their financial problems are a result of the European ban, not bad agriculture and trade policy, according to Steve Suppan, an agricultural trade analyst at the Institute for Agriculture and Trade Policy.

Seeking to Stifle Knowledge

Monsanto and other biotech advocates strongly object to any requirements that food be labeled as containing genetically modified agricultural products.

But even the most ardent defender of free markets would acknowledge that if markets are going to work properly, all the participants must be fully informed. How can King (or Queen) Consumer decide what to buy if the ingredients are secret?

The World Trade Organization decision also nullifies democracy at all levels by attempting to override decisions by individual European countries, by the European Union and by the international community (in its Biosafety Protocol).

At the WTO, the principle is trade, especially the interests of corporations like Monsanto, over everything else. That principle and power is bad for consumers and citizens everywhere.

> "[The Doha Round] should be carefully constructed to ensure that . . . developing countries will retain the policy flexibility necessary to . . . increase food security."

The WTO Can Play an Important Role in Establishing Global Food Security

Sandra Polaski

Sandra Polaski is a senior associate and director of the Trade, Equity, and Development Program at the Carnegie Endowment for International Peace. In the following viewpoint, she reviews the issues at stake in the Doha Round of World Trade Organization trade negotiations in light of rising food prices and their impact on global poverty. Polaski then argues that the WTO can help ensure food security by ensuring that the Doha Round allow developing countries adequate policy flexibility so that they can build up their own agricultural sectors, increase food supply in the medium and long term, and shield the poor from market failures that can affect their survival.

Sandra Polaski, "Rising Food Prices, Poverty, and the Doha Round," Carnegie Endowment for International Peace, May 2008, pp. 9–13. © 2008 Carnegie Endowment for International Peace. Reproduced by permission.

As you read, consider the following questions:

1. How do experts expect that a Doha settlement would impact food prices in the short term, according to Polaski?

2. How does the author believe that many developing countries can reduce poverty and increase food security?

3. What effect does domestic and export subsidies have on farmers in developing countries, according to Polaski?

It is generally acknowledged by experts that a Doha settlement would have no short-term impact on food prices. The tariff changes and other rules of a final deal will not begin to take effect until after the agreement is concluded, ratified by member states, and comes into force, a process that will take several years. Countries will then begin to phase in agreed changes over a number of years. The prior Uruguay Round, for example, allowed countries ten years to implement commitments. The trade negotiations, however, are not aimed at the short term. The rules and tariffs negotiated will prevail for the foreseeable future, until changed by some yet unscheduled future round of global trade talks. As a result, the Doha Round must be assessed for its medium and long term implications.

What Doha Can Accomplish

During the six years since the launch of the Doha Round [in 2001], numerous general equilibrium studies have been undertaken to simulate its potential impacts. All studies have found that a Doha package that includes reductions in domestic agricultural subsidies, export subsidies, and tariffs will raise food prices modestly on global markets. These studies have also reached the common conclusion that most developing countries will see some benefits from the Round, although net food importing countries including Bangladesh and many sub-Saharan African countries are likely to be net losers because of the increased cost of food.

Public discourse on the link between rising food prices and the Doha Round has sometimes been based on a mistaken belief that a conclusion to the negotiations is needed to lower prices by requiring countries to cut tariffs. However all countries currently have the right to lower the tariffs they actually apply—including to zero—at any time. WTO membership only obligates countries not to *raise* tariffs beyond levels agreed to in previous rounds of negotiations (these are called "bound" rates). In practice, many developing countries have already cut tariffs in the context of rising food prices to bring immediate relief to their consumers, including the poor.

There is a large gap between bound and applied tariff rates, particularly in agriculture, and it is more common for developing countries to maintain such gaps. A major reason they have sought to maintain higher bound rates while sometimes applying low tariffs in practice is their need to deal with the volatility of agricultural prices. . . . When global food prices are high, as now, governments have the ability to lower tariffs. When global food prices fall (as they have and will again), governments can raise tariffs back up to the bound level to shield their farmers from sharp drops in income. This flexibility is particularly desirable going forward, when two factors may increase price volatility. First, scientists predict more extreme and variable weather as a result of climate change, which could lead to more frequent supply shortfalls. The other factor is the increasing role played by futures markets for agricultural commodities. . . . Like other financial markets, they are driven as much or more by speculation, expectations, and herd behavior than by underlying fundamentals and so tend to be much more volatile than actual supply and demand.

Increasing Food Security

In the long term, reducing poverty and increasing food security will require many developing countries to expand agricultural production and improve domestic agricultural markets. There are a number of issues still under negotiation in the Doha Round that will affect the ability of governments to achieve these goals and manage food price changes in the future.

The domestic and export subsidies provided by the United States, the European Union, and some other wealthy countries to their farmers have the effect of inducing greater supply than market prices would warrant and allowing excess production to be sold on world markets at prices below production costs. This has reduced global food prices over recent decades, which was seen as positive by some net food importing countries. However it has hurt farmers in developing countries who cannot compete with subsidized exports in global markets. For subsistence and small scale farmers, it has displaced or lowered prices for their output in their domestic markets, thereby driving them off the land or into poverty.

A similar effect is caused by in-kind food aid, which is the main form of food assistance provided by the United States. While most other wealthy countries have shifted to providing food aid by purchasing from farmers in countries targeted for assistance or in neighboring countries, the United States still does so by shipping its excess domestic supplies to destination countries, displacing production or depressing prices there.

Agricultural subsidies and in-kind food aid by wealthy countries have discouraged production and investment in developing country agriculture. The resulting shortfall has emerged starkly as global food demand has risen. Thus, while reducing these agricultural subsidies and constraining in-kind food aid will increase prices modestly in the short run, it is a necessary correction to global agricultural market distortions and an essential part of the Doha deal if developing countries are to build up their own agricultural sectors and increase food supply in the medium and long term.

Special Products

Earlier in the Doha Round a framework agreement was reached to allow developing countries to shield some agricultural products, designated special products, from tariff reductions in order to address the livelihood security, food security, and rural development concerns that have been discussed above. Negotiations continue on how extensive these exceptions will be. A large group of developing countries known as the G33 has proposed that twenty percent of tariff lines should be subjected to lesser or no tariff cuts based on these considerations. The United States and some other countries have sought to sharply limit the number of eligible tariff lines and to require other constraints in the designation of special products.

The outcome will determine how much flexibility developing country governments will have to provide some price continuity as a long term incentive to their farmers to increase production. It will also influence the degree to which they will be able to shield poor farmers and rural communities from high levels of risk or periods of depressed prices that they are ill-prepared to absorb.

While the G33 has been outspoken throughout the negotiations about the need for this policy flexibility, the recent price volatility and supply shortfalls on global food markets have convinced some other developing countries that they need to consider ways to achieve greater domestic production in order to improve food security and reduce vulnerability to global markets. Many African countries in particular have the land and labor endowments needed for increased food production if they invest in irrigation and other rural infrastructure and can induce farmers to invest and increase production. Even if they are able to mobilize resources for public investments, greater effort by farmers and more private investment will not be forthcoming unless governments retain the tariff flexibility to shield farmers, particularly small and vulnerable ones, from the worst of global market volatility and negative price shocks. A robust outcome on special products would be needed.

As already discussed, the impact of food prices on poverty and income distribution varies widely among countries and for different agricultural crops within countries. As a result, the decisions on how to select special products must be left to developing country governments themselves. Efforts in the negotiations to severely limit the number of special products or to impose restrictions on their selection would undermine the ability of developing country governments to balance the needs of rural and urban poor while addressing food supply and longer term rural development. Decisions on such fundamental issues must be left to governments that are accountable to their populations, not to negotiators seeking to maximize profits for their own commercial farmers or to dispute settlement panels that have no such accountability.

Special Safeguard Mechanism

Developing countries also seek a special safeguard mechanism that would permit them to raise tariffs in response to agricultural price drops or import surges. While the special products exceptions discussed above would provide some policy space for developing countries to address medium term food security and livelihood concerns and long term rural development strategies, a safeguard mechanism would still be needed to address short term volatility in food markets. As noted, food prices have always been volatile and volatility is likely to increase due to climate change and increased use of commodities as investments and hedges. Small producers in developing countries are in no position to bear the risk of sharp price and supply swings.

The special safeguard mechanism must be easy to use, allow developing countries to respond swiftly to market disruptions, and be available for relatively small disruptions. In the simulations we performed of the impact of changing rice prices in India, a twenty-five percent decrease in rice prices imposes losses on poor households almost as large as a fifty percent decrease. A current proposal that would require import prices to fall by as much as thirty percent compared to the average price for the previous three years (the "trigger price") before the safeguard mechanism could be employed would vitiate [make ineffective] this important tool. Another current proposal would limit a responding tariff increase to one-half of the difference between the lower import price and the trigger price. The practical effect would be to require that half of global market disruptions be absorbed by poor farmers in affected countries. The proposal should be abandoned. Consideration must also be given to the situation of developing countries with low bound tariffs, which might need to raise them well above current bound levels to have an effect on import surges and negative price shocks.

A Broad Range of Policy Tools

The policy tools needed to address the current food crisis cover a broad range. They include immediate assistance for the poor and hungry and dramatically increased investment in developing country agriculture by the international financial institutions, wealthy country development agencies, and developing country governments. Financial regulators should turn their attention to financial markets in agricultural commodities, which show signs of the speculation, mania, and overshooting that have resulted in ongoing crises in global finance and some housing markets. As painful and destructive as those crises have been, they pale by comparison with the threat of serious market failure in the case of food.

Trade policy also has a role to play. Many developing countries aspire to link their agricultural producers to larger regional and global markets as they gain the capacity to compete against more efficient producers under conditions of volatility. However, trade liberalization that removes flexibility from the hands of developing country governments prematurely or leads them to rely on global food markets and not invest in their own agricultural sectors has proven to be short-sighted. In the case of the Doha Round, a quick conclusion would not influence the current spike in food prices. Instead, an agreement should be carefully constructed to ensure that in the future, developing countries will retain the policy flexibility necessary to develop and provide appropriate incentives to their domestic agricultural sectors, to increase food security, and to shield the poor from market failures that can affect their very survival.

| *"WTO ... never anticipated that export controls might create [food] scarcities."*

Unfair Agricultural Policies Have Led to Global Food Insecurity

Swaminathan S. Anklesaria Aiyar

Aiyar is a research fellow at the U.S. think tank the Cato Institute and a columnist for the Times of India. *The author argues that export controls create food scarcities.*

As you read, consider the following questions:

1. According to the United Nations Food and Agriculture Organization, as cited by the author, what should be the world production of cereal in 2008?

2. How much of the U.S. corn crop does Aiyar say has been diverted to ethanol?

3. What was the result of the worldwide popularity of biofuels, according to the author?

Swaminathan S. Anklesaria Aiyar, "Against the Grain," *American Spectator*, June 13, 2008. Reproduced by permission.

International rice and wheat prices have doubled or tripled in the last two years [2006–08], but world grain production will reach a record high this year [2008]. So how come millions are falling into poverty and starting food riots across the world? The answer lies not in any outsized surge in world demand or fall in world supply, but in the fact that several countries have imposed duties, quotas and outright bans on agricultural exports. This has reduced the amount of grain available for world trade.

The United Nations Food and Agriculture Organization (FAO) estimates that world production of cereals was a record 2,108 million tons in 2007, and will hit a new record of 2,164 million tons in 2008. Rice production will rise by 7.3 million tons and wheat by 41 million tons. World cereal consumption has been growing slightly faster (3%) than production (2%) for a decade, so global stocks have fallen to 405 million tons. But this is not a disaster scenario, and it hardly explains skyrocketing prices.

Biofuels Contribute to Food Insecurity

In the U.S., one-fifth of the corn crop has been diverted to ethanol, and in Europe, some vegetable oil has been diverted to biodiesel. These ill-conceived policies have induced farmers to switch significant acreage from wheat to corn, soybeans and rapeseed, but world wheat output has nevertheless risen from 596.5 million tons in 2006 to an estimated 647.3 million tons in 2008. Corn-based ethanol cannot explain the runaway increase in the price of rice, which grows in very different conditions.

Biofuels caused an initial spike in prices, which then led to panic, export protectionism and speculation in commodities futures—and these latter factors have increased prices much further. To protect domestic consumers from rising world prices, dozens of governments have curbed the export of rice and wheat—principally Argentina, Brazil, Russia, China, India, Ukraine, Vietnam, Cambodia, Pakistan, Egypt, and Indonesia.

Export controls have reduced the amount of rice and wheat available for world trade. The FAO estimates that world trade in rice will fall from 34.7 million tons in 2007 to 28.7 million tons in 2008, and trade in wheat from 113 million tons to 106 million tons. Actual trade may fall even more, as more and more countries impose export controls. Absent these limitations, it would be inconceivable for trade in grain to contract so sharply after record world harvests.

Countries limiting exports hope to reduce hoarding, which could send prices even higher. India has set limits on the stocks that each trader can hold.

Policies Are Harmful

But countries imposing export controls, have, in effect, become hoarders themselves, creating an artificial scarcity in the world market, and an artificially high world price. Farmers know what their crops could fetch on the world market, so they demand higher prices at home. And around and around we go.

This has eerie similarities to the Great Depression, when many countries resorted to import protection to protect jobs at home, and simultaneously devalued their currencies to try and push up exports. Yet the Great Depression got worse, thanks to what [economist] John Maynard Keynes called the fallacy of composition.

If one country alone resorts to import protection and devaluation, it can temporarily increase jobs. But at a global level, one country's exports are another's imports. If all countries reduce their imports, they unwittingly end up reducing their exports, too. And job losses get worse.

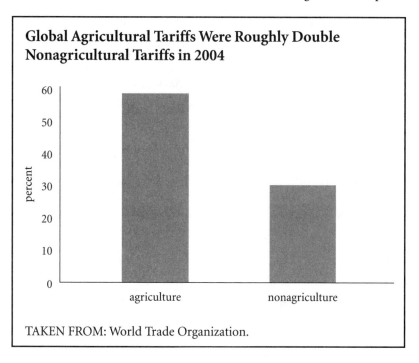

Global Agricultural Tariffs Were Roughly Double Nonagricultural Tariffs in 2004

TAKEN FROM: World Trade Organization.

Today, each country wants to curb agricultural exports and stimulate imports to reduce prices. But if every country limits exports, the result is a decline in world imports, so prices rise instead of falling.

WTO Has Caused Problems

Solving the problem may require coordinated international action. After the Great Depression, the world community created the Global Agreement on Tariffs and Trade—which later morphed into the World Trade Organization—to negotiate simultaneous cuts in import barriers by major trading powers. This coordinated approach thwarted free riders, and gradually gained acceptance by all.

WTO rules permit food export limitations. In the Doha Round of trade negotiations, WTO has sought to reduce agricultural subsidies causing excess production. It never anticipated that export controls might create scarcities.

The new developments may improve the prospects of the Doha Round. But quick action is needed to tackle rising hunger. The WTO should convene an emergency meeting for countries to jointly reduce export controls. Even modest concessions can be in exporters' self-interest, as they would cause world prices to fall sharply, and thus ease domestic price pressures.

The terrible irony is that world grain production will be at a record high in 2008. People are hungry, and it's not because there isn't enough food to go around.

Periodical Bibliography

Walden Bello   "Manufacturing a Food Crisis," *Nation*, May
                        15, 2008.

Jake Caldwell   "Climate Change and International
                        Competitiveness," Center for American
                        Progress, April 7, 2009.
                        www.americanprogress.org.

Mark Engler   "The WTO in Hong Kong," *Counterpunch*,
                        December 16, 2005.

Hilary Hylton   "Keeping U.S. Turtles Out of China," *Time*,
                        May 8, 2007.

Sallie James   "Crisis Averted? How Government Actions
                        Keep Food Prices High," Cato Institute,
                        December 8, 2008. www.cato.org.

Andrew Leonard   "Peru's Bio-Piracy Gestapo Terrorizes the
                        West," *Salon*, December 15, 2005.
                        www.salon.com.

Rich Lowry   "Stolen Property," *National Review*, April 18,
                        2006.

Bill Powell   "A Losing Battle Against Chinese Piracy," *Time*,
                        April 10, 2007.

Steve Rayner   "Why We Can't Agree," *Newsweek*, September
                        15, 2003.

Stephan Spruiell   "Loopy Loopholes," *National Review*, December
                        13, 2005.

Michael A. Tew and   "Who Needs Foreign Investment?" *American
Alexandra V. Preate   Spectator*, March 24, 2007.

Brian Tokar   "WTO v. Europe," *Counterpunch*, February 18,
                        2006.

Mark Weisbrot   "Climate Change and Intellectual Property
                        Rights?" *Counterpunch*, May 22, 2009.

OPPOSING
VIEWPOINTS®
SERIES

CHAPTER 4

How Should the United States Relate to the WTO?

Chapter Preface

One of the main duties of the World Trade Organization (WTO) is settling trade disputes between countries through the organization's trade dispute settlement system, known as the Dispute Settlement Body (DSB). When countries join the WTO, they agree to abide by the organization's rules—one of which is that if they believe that another country is in violation of a trade agreement or WTO trade rules, they will not take action on their own, but rather adjudicate the matter in the DSB. Many cases are settled before they can be heard in the DSB, through consultations and mediations.

The DSB is tasked with overseeing the entire dispute settlement process. It also has the authority to implement rules and recommendations, adopt panel and Appellate Body reports, and adjust member obligations under certain circumstances. Decisions made by the panel can be appealed to the Appellate Body.

The WTO trade dispute settlement process is a complicated one. If a WTO member country accuses another one of violating an agreement, it first calls for consultations with the accused, which should last for sixty days. If consultations fail, the accuser may request a panel to adjudicate the dispute. The WTO secretariat will then appoint three members to the panel, and the panel will receive written and oral arguments. All proceedings are confidential. The panel has six months to make a decision and write a report, which is distributed first to the pertinent parties, and then to all WTO members. A decision can be appealed by either party on matters of law and legal interpretation, and an Apellate Report will be distributed in ninety days.

The DSB then monitors the compliance of both parties to the panel's decision. If a member fails to comply with the ruling, compensation may be awarded to one party from another, based on DSB ruling. Many critics argue that "retaliatory measures" like this are a weak mechanism to try to gain justice. It is one thing for an economically strong country like the United States to extract compensation from a weaker country, but when used by a weaker one against a stronger one, compensation is often ignored. In some instances, it has been the United States that has ignored WTO trade settlement dispute rulings when they have not been in its favor.

Supporters of the WTO and the rule of law argue that by joining the WTO, countries have to adhere to the organization's trade dispute settlement system. No matter the size or economic power of the country, they are subject to the same rules and decisions as all member countries and must abide by even unfavorable DSB rulings.

The debate over the efficacy of the WTO trade dispute settlement system is one of the issues discussed in the following chapter, which debates how the United States should relate to the WTO.

> "What [the United States] should do is
> to bring our law and conduct into com-
> pliance with our international legal ob-
> ligations ... rather than try to renege
> on its promises."

The United States Must Comply with WTO Rulings Against It

Joseph Weiler

Joseph Weiler is a law professor and the director of the Jean Monnet Center for International and Regional Economic Law and Justice at New York University. In the following testimony before the House Committee on the Judiciary, he stresses the necessity of the United States' honoring and respecting of its international legal obligations to the World Trade Organization, even if the United States opposes the decisions. Weiler acknowledges that many observers believe that the United States is trying to cynically manipulate the system to its favor, which threatens the precarious nature of international trade agreements.

Joseph Weiler, "Testimony of Joseph H. H. Weiler, Professor of Law, Director Jean Monnet Center for International and Regional Economic Law and Justice, New York University School of Law," Testimony Before the U.S. House of Representatives Committee on the Judiciary Hearing on Establishing Consistent Policies in the Context of Online Wagers, November 15, 2007. Reproduced by permission.

As you read, consider the following questions:

1. How is the United States regulating or banning in a discriminatory manner, according to Weiler?

2. Why should U.S. citizens and Congress be upset with the move of the executive branch to withdraw its commitment on Internet regulation, in the author's opinion?

3. What is the Charming Betsy doctrine, as defined by Weiler?

My name is Joseph Weiler. . . . One area of my expertise is the law of the World Trade Organization. I have served on occasion as a WTO panel member. . . .

Recently I have been retained, and continue to be retained, by several law firms whose clients include individuals and corporations who have been indicted or are threatened by the US under the Wire Act and other related acts for offering remote Internet betting services from outside the United States. I was asked to provide them with expert advice on, *inter alia* [among other things], the compatibility of such indictments with US international legal obligations and more generally with the compatibility of the overall US ban on remote betting from providers located outside the US in countries which are Member States of the WTO.

In my testimony to Congress today I want to summarize my principal conclusions and recommendations.

Role of WTO

The United States is a founding Member of the GATT [General Agreement on Tariffs and Trade], and a founding and prominent Member of the WTO. One of the Agreements which come under the umbrella of the WTO is the GATS—The General Agreement on Trade in Services, under which a Member such as the United States *may* if it so wishes, open certain economic sectors to service providers from other Members. The incentive for a Member such as the US to open up such sectors is self-interest: It is part of complex negotiations whereby other countries may offer similar commitments in respect of US service providers. Additionally, opening up internal services to outside providers may be considered in the interest of US consumers—offering them more choice and enhancing competition which produce efficiency and lower prices. A country is not obliged to give such commitments but once it does it is obliged to respect them—since other countries adjust their economies in view of such commitments and individual corporations and investors will gear their economic activities based on such commitments and promise of access.

The Origins of Dispute

The United States voluntarily gave a legally binding Commitment in respect of "Recreational, Culture and Sporting Services," which have been held to include gambling and betting services.

Notwithstanding its clear international obligation to offer access to the thriving remote betting industry within the United States to providers from other WTO Members, the United States has used the Wire Act and other related Acts criminally to indict and even convict individuals and corporations and effectively to shut out all such access to outside providers.

Antigua brought a case against the US in the WTO challenging the legality of the US conduct. The United States sought to defend the legality of its conduct before all judicial instances of the WTO. It has lost, comprehensively, in all such proceedings. Its conduct was held to be illegal by a WTO Panel, the WTO Appellate Body (the supreme judicial instance of the WTO) and a subsequent Compliance Panel.

U.S. Response

In face of such conclusive holding of illegality the US has decided not to appeal the final decision of the Compliance Panel. Instead the US has taken steps to withdraw its GATS commitment in this area. This might be regarded and is regarded by many as a cynical manipulation of the system—you lose the game, so you try and change the rules. It also charts a way and creates a political precedent which might harm US interests when other countries emulate such behavior. Be that as it may, it constitutes a ringing admission by the United States of the illegality of its actions to date.

And yet, the US Executive Branch persists in maintaining indictments and threatening indictments that are based on internationally tainted Acts and conduct. In what is in my view a particularly astonishing approach, the Executive Branch is persisting in a policy which includes prosecutions against individuals the legality of whose activities were covered and guaranteed by the international legal obligations of the United States, and is simply seeking to defend itself by relying on the ground that its illegal actions are shielded by the Uruguay Round Implementing Act from suits by individuals in domestic US courts. The approach of the Executive Branch amounts to the following: "What we are doing may be illegal under international law, but you, the individuals cannot do anything about it, because under our reading of the Uruguay Round Agreement Act we are immune." Even if the URAA gave such immunity to the Executive Branch—which I do not believe to be the case—this approach amounts to a spectacular contempt for the rule of international law and to American notions of fairness and justice.

Clearing Up Misunderstandings

Let me now dispel some misunderstandings surrounding this saga. The WTO regime (of which the United States is one of the principal architects) is often depicted as encroaching on US "sovereignty" and internal autonomy in an unacceptable way. What, it is sometimes asked, if the United States came to the conclusion that, say, Internet betting posed specific risks to consumers which require regulation or even banning of such forms of betting?

Does the WTO prohibit the US from taking action to protect against such risks? The answer is a resounding no. If such risks exist the US would have full legal authority under the GATS to regulate the industry to protect it against such risks. If it considered it wise it could even impose a ban. But what it cannot do is to regulate or ban in a discriminatory manner. Under its WTO obligations it cannot regulate or ban in a manner which slyly supports and allows domestic providers of remote betting but, for example, bans suppliers from WTO partners. All legal instances in the WTO found that this is exactly what the US is doing today. The WTO found, that whereas the US was trying to justify its ban on outside providers of remote betting services by considerations of public policy and public order it allowed at the very same time within the USA the operation of

> ". . . substantial and even prominent businesses, with, collectively, thousands of employees and apparently tens of thousands of clients, paying taxes or generating revenue for government owners, having traded openly for up to 30 years and in some cases even operating television channels. . . . The evidence regarding the suppliers demonstrates the existence of a flourishing remote account wagering industry on horse racing in the United States operating in ostensible legality."

The conduct of the Executive Branch in banning outside providers is not just discriminatory and thus in violation of the WTO, but one cannot escape the suspicion that it might be motivated in part by a protection of special interests within the United States rather than protection of consumers.

Conduct of the Executive Branch

The conduct of the Executive Branch is harmful to the United States in many ways.

Our economy relies more and more on a robust exporting sector—both in goods and services. The WTO including the

GATT and GATS are the principal legal framework which guarantees US businesses a discrimination-free environment in which to sell their products and services in other WTO countries. Imagine that a foreign country took a commitment which, say, allowed American hospitals and doctors access to offer medical services. Imagine further that based on that commitment the US hospitals and doctors began offering services in a WTO Member. Imagine now that this country failed to live up to its commitment and imprisoned American doctors on the ground that a national law forbade the offering of such services to doctors not trained in the host country. We would be rightly outraged. We would be even more outraged if that country turned to the American doctors and said: though we acknowledge that our actions are in violation of our agreement, according to our internal law, you have no recourse. You sit in jail. But what would we say if that country turned around and said—We are only following the example of the United States of America. Our outrage would at this point turn not against such a country but against our own Executive Branch.

We should be equally concerned by the move of the Executive Branch to withdraw its commitment. What it should do is to bring our law and conduct into compliance with our international legal obligations on which many countries and individuals have relied rather than try to renege on its promises. This is not simply or even primarily a moralistic point. Our country is the trendsetter and leader in so many international arenas. Whether we like it or not, *we lead by example*. As our economy moves increasingly towards a high tech, knowledge-based service-oriented model and as we realize that our future prosperity will depend increasingly on tapping into export markets, notably the huge emerging markets such as China and India, is it really in our self interest to teach this particular example? When you are caught denying access or discriminating against American businesses in violation of your GATS or GATT obligations, rather than complying, simply withdraw your commitment and change your promise?

The United States justly used to enjoy a world reputation as a champion of liberty, rights and the rule of law. I think it is acknowledged by all political forces that in recent times this reputation has been seriously diminished compromising American leadership and American interests. In some areas, notably in the area of the war on terror and national security, there might be a feeling that existing rules of international law compromise the ability of the United States effectively to defend itself. I make no pronouncement on that. But if this is the case, it would seem to me that in all other areas, where national security is not involved, this country would be well served if its Executive Branch was particularly vigilant and scrupulous in observing the rule of law, which includes a respect for international legal obligations. This is, too, in the interest of the United States. It should be recalled that United States signed and supported the WTO Dispute Resolution Understanding which provides, *inter alia*, in Article 17.14

> An Appellate Body report shall be adopted by the DSB [Dispute Settlement Body] and *unconditionally accepted by the parties to the dispute* unless the DSB decides by consensus not to adopt the Appellate Body report within 30 days following its circulation to the Members. (Emphasis added.)

Article 21.1 of the DSU provides in turn:

> Prompt compliance with recommendations or rulings of the DSB is essential in order to ensure effective resolution of disputes to the benefit of all Members.

It should also be recalled that the United States is often on the winning side of trade disputes, and when it is on the winning side it insists vigorously that its trading partners faithfully comply with their legal obligations.

U.S. Dispute over Meat Hormones

To give but one example: In its famous dispute with the European Union as regards exportation of meat hormones, the US won its case. Here are the words of the representative of the US in the WTO:

> The representative of the United States said that this was an important juncture in the dispute settlement process. Her delegation welcomed the [European Union's] statement. It was important for the integrity and viability of the dispute settlement mechanism that Members complied with the DSB's recommendations. In this case, the Communities' obligations were clear. In accordance with the rulings, the ban had not been supported by scientific evidence nor by any of the risk assessments presented during the proceedings. All the risk assessments that had been conducted had proved that the six hormones in question were safe. This meant that compliance with the DSB's recommendations required the Communities to remove the ban on the importation of meat produced with the use of any of the six hormones to promote growth.

The matter this Committee is considering is not about National Security; the US Executive Branch is the custodian of the United States national interest. It is not in American interest to weaken the ability of the United States to insist on prompt compliance with WTO rulings by others.

When a Member fails to comply with a decision of the WTO Appellate Body and Dispute Settlement Body, it opens itself to trade sanctions by the winning country in the form of withdrawal of concessions. This has been interpreted by some to suggest that as long as the US was willing to submit itself to such sanctions, it was discharging its obligations under the WTO system. This is an utter misconception of the system. The withdrawal of concessions is meant to be a sanction and incentive for a recalcitrant Member to fulfill its obligation, not an indulgence you buy to expiate your wrongdoing. To argue otherwise would be the equivalent of a rich man claiming that as long he was willing to pay the fine, he was under no legal obligation to move the car he parked in front of a fire hydrant.

U.S. Must Honor Obligations

This Committee is not a court of law so I will spare it a lengthy legal analysis concerning the question whether or not individuals may rely in their defense against the indictments brought against them on the fact that the Acts on which such indictments have been brought have been found to be in violation of the US legal obligations when applied to individuals supplying remote betting services from other WTO Members. Some language in the Uruguay Round Agreement Act notwithstanding I think there are weighty legal arguments that individuals should not be denied, *in defending themselves*, the ability to argue that Congress did not intend in approving US participation in the WTO, that prosecutorial discretion should be exercised in a manner which would bring the United States into violation of its international legal obligations. There is, however, one crucial point which should be of interest to this Committee. In many of its utterances the Executive Branch has taken the position that it is defending the "sovereignty" of the United States as a whole, and that in its conduct in this matter it is executing the will of Congress. I respectfully and vigorously dispute both these propositions. When a country solemnly adopts an international legal obligation and then honors that obligation it does not compromise its sovereignty—it manifests its sovereignty. For generations the United States has taken the view that all Congressional Acts should, if at all possible, be interpreted and applied in such a way as to respect international obligations solemnly undertaken by this country. This is called the Charming Betsy doctrine. We expect the same from all other countries. It is possible to interpret both the Uruguay Round Agreement Act (taking the US into the WTO) and the Statutes under which the Executive Branch is seeking to ban remote betting from service suppliers located in our WTO partners, in a manner which would respect American international legal obligation and commitment to the rule of law. The Executive Branch is doing no service to the US by violating these obligations, and laying the responsibility at the feet of Congress. Congress should not allow such.

As I indicated above, it is clear that remote betting over the Internet does pose various legitimate concerns. There are potential hazards to, for example, consumers which do not exist in on-site gambling. If the United States were to adopt a "prohibition mentality" the WTO would not prevent the US from banning all such betting, provided such a ban could be justified on grounds of public policy and public morality and was applicable to *all* remote betting, internal and external. I do not think such a total ban is either wise or likely. The alternative is to adopt a regulatory regime which would address the hazards of remote betting and would apply with no discrimination both to domestic and foreign service providers from our WTO partners. In this way the US would both address its legitimate social concerns and respect its international legal obligations.

*"The World Trade Organization is a di-
rect attack on U.S. sovereignty."*

The United States Should Not Allow the WTO to Infringe on Its National Sovereignty

Phyllis Schlafly

Phyllis Schlafly is an author and conservative columnist and commentator. In the following viewpoint, she bemoans the World Trade Organization decision that rules that Antigua and Barbuda can violate American copyrights and trademarks in order to punish the United States for laws prohibiting Internet gambling. Schlafly believes these WTO rulings to be a direct attack on U.S. sovereignty and should not be tolerated.

As you read, consider the following questions:

1. Why did Congress pass the Unlawful Internet Gambling Enforcement Act in 2006, according to the author?

2. According to Schlafly, how is the United States responding to the WTO decision?

Phyllis Schlafly, "World Trade Organization Is No Friend to U.S.," *Townhall.com*, January 7, 2008. Reproduced by permission.

3. The WTO has ruled against the United States in how many out of forty-seven major cases, according to the author?

"WTO" now stands for "World Trade Outrage" rather than its original name, World Trade Organization. The World Trade Organization just ruled that the Caribbean nation of Antigua and Barbuda can freely violate American copyrights and trademarks in order to punish the United States for laws prohibiting Internet gambling.

Congress passed the Unlawful Internet Gambling Enforcement Act in 2006 after finding that "Internet gambling is a growing cause of debt collection problems for insured depository institutions and the consumer credit industry." The social and financial costs of gambling would be greatly increased if the United States permits Internet gambling.

The World Trade Organization ordered this punishment because it says U.S. laws interfere with free trade in "recreational services." The foreign tribunal ranks free trade as more important than the intellectual property rights Americans have enjoyed since the U.S. Constitution was written.

The World Trade Organization's 88-page decision issued in December [2007] contained the panel's remarkable admission that "we feel we are on shaky grounds." But that didn't stop the Geneva tribunal from issuing its ruling anyway.

Protecting Sovereignty

The United States has every right as a nation to protect its people against the corruption and loss of wealth that result from gambling on the Internet. It is shocking for an unelected foreign tribunal to tell the U.S. House of Representatives, the U.S. Senate and the president of the United States that they lack the power to protect U.S. citizens.

Even American supremacist judges would not have the nerve to authorize stealing copyrights and trademarks as a remedy for one side in an unrelated dispute. But the World Trade Organization granted what has been called a "piracy permit" that allows a small Caribbean nation to "pirate," or steal, U.S. property rights.

The response in Washington was to announce an attempt to revise the conditions under which the United States joined the World Trade Organization in 1994. That's a non-starter because these changes in the World Trade Organization treaty would require the approval of all 151 members, most of whom don't like the U.S. anyway.

The World Trade Organization has ruled against the United States in 40 out of 47 major cases, and against the U.S. in 30 out of 33 trade remedies cases. After the World Trade Organization ruled that the U.S. cannot divert tariff revenue to U.S. companies that are injured by foreign subsidies to their competitors, Vice President Dick Cheney provided the tie-breaking vote in the Senate on Dec. 21, 2005, to kowtow to the World Trade Organization.

WTO Rulings Undermine U.S. Laws

For many years, opponents of the World Trade Organization have predicted that this foreign bureaucracy would massively interfere with U.S. sovereignty. This new ruling is crazy, unjust and impertinent, but without a lot of public protest, it looks unlikely that our "free trade" president or Congress will do anything to protect U.S. citizens from the World Trade Organization.

How is a foreign tribunal in Geneva able to put the United States in such a box? It's because the internationalist free-trade lobby cooked up a sleazy deal to force the World Trade Organization on Americans in 1994 during the week after Thanksgiving, when Americans were preoccupied with Christmas shopping and festivities.

Implications of the WTO Ruling

The implications of the [antigambling] case go far beyond Antigua, a nation of 69,000. That's because, instead
of rewriting its gambling laws, the U.S. rewrote its trade
rules to remove the issue from the WTO's jurisdiction.
The prospect that other nations, including China, may
take a similar tack if cases don't go their way has spooked
the international trade community.

"This is by far the most significant WTO case ever,"
says Naotaka Matsukata, a policy adviser in Washington
with Alston and Bird LLP and a former U.S. trade official.

Lorraine Woellert, Bloomberg,
December 17, 2007. www.bloomberg.com.

U.S. and WTO

The deal to lock the United States into [the] World Trade Organization consisted of three parts. First, the 14-page World
Trade Organization agreement was surreptitiously added, without debate or publicity, to the 22,000-page revision of the
General Agreement on Tariffs and Trade, implementing legislation, and was voted on under "fast track" rules that allowed
no amendments or changes, severely limited debate, and forbade any filibuster.

Second, the Treaty Clause in the U.S. Constitution for ratification of treaties was ignored, and World Trade Organization
was declared passed by Congress as a non-treaty. Third, the
General Agreement on Tariffs and Trade/World Trade Organization agreement was passed in the December lame-duck ses-
sion with the votes of dozens of Congressmen who were look-

ing for lucrative jobs representing foreign interests because they had already been defeated in the Republican landslide of November 1994.

The World Trade Organization is not "free trade" at all, but is a supra-national body in Geneva that sets, manages and enforces World Trade Organization-made rules to govern global trade. The World Trade Organization includes a one country–one vote legislature of 151 nations (the United States has the same one vote as Cuba), an unelected multinational bureaucracy, and a Dispute Settlement Board that deliberates and votes in secret and whose decisions cannot be appealed or vetoed.

WTO Is an Attack on U.S. Sovereignty

The World Trade Organization is a direct attack on U.S. sovereignty because it claims it can force any nation to change its laws to comply with World Trade Organization rulings. Article XVI, paragraph 4, states: "Each Member shall ensure the conformity of its laws, regulations, and administrative procedures with its obligations." The World Trade Organization has the final say about whether U.S. laws meet World Trade Organization requirements.

In this presidential season, the World Trade Organization should make easy target practice for any candidate to speak up and defend U.S. sovereignty against globalists who, under the mantra of "free trade," willingly allow the World Trade Organization to say which laws the U.S. may or may not adopt.

"A helpful first step in restoring credibility about the United States' commitment to free markets would be to cease filing complaints with WTO and NAFTA panels and to acquiesce with all decisions adjudicated by those panels."

The United States Should Obey WTO Trade Settlement Decisions

Mark W. Hendrickson

Mark W. Hendrickson is a faculty member, economist, and contributing scholar with the Center for Vision and Values at Grove City College in Pennsylvania. In the following viewpoint, he contends that many foreigners view the United States with mistrust and contempt because of the country's cavalier and cynical approach to trade agreements and regulations. Hendrickson states that the United States must acquiesce to all WTO decisions and rulings in order to gain back credibility in the world community on the subject of trade.

Mark W. Hendrickson, "Globalization in a Nutshell," *Frontpagemag.com*, April 3, 2007. Reproduced by permission of Center for the Study of Popular Culture.

As you read, consider the following questions:

1. How did President George W. Bush defy the WTO, according to the author?

2. What is the so-called "Byrd Amendment," as defined by Hendrickson?

3. What does the author cite as a consequence for U.S. heavy-handed actions regarding trade issues?

The U.S. government, under Democrat and Republican presidents alike, strove mightily for the creation and adoption of NAFTA and the WTO, the two principal trade agreements adopted by the United States in the last 15 years. The American goal had been to establish a durable framework for peaceful trade relations. However, once those agreements went into effect, it seemed that politicians of both parties vied with each other to see who could do the most to defy those agreements, thereby aligning themselves with the anti-globalizers.

NAFTA and the WTO

Republican President George W. Bush defied the WTO by imposing ... special tariffs on foreign-produced steel for 20 months in 2002 and 2003. Bush also targeted Canadian producers of soft lumber, eventually extracting four or five billion dollars of illegal tariffs from them in defiance of multiple NAFTA rulings (tariffs that effectively raised the average price of building a new home in the United States by $1,000).

Not to be outdone, Democratic Sen. Robert Byrd of West Virginia succeeded in pushing the Continued Dumping and Subsidy Offset Act of 2000 through Congress. The so-called "Byrd Amendment" amounted to a virtual declaration of a trade war against foreign producers. It empowered domestic firms to file charges of unfair trade practices against their foreign competitors, and then, without an audit or any other serious investigation of the validity of their claims, Uncle Sam would collect tariffs on the targeted imports and give those funds directly to the U.S. firms that filed the complaints against their foreign competitors. Multiple WTO rulings denounced this financial piracy, but Congress resisted abolishing the Byrd Amendment for several years until American firms were lining up to file claims for more money than the entire U.S. gross domestic product, at which point Congress finally pulled the plug on this corporate welfare scheme.

The flagrant flouting of the very trade agreements that U.S. leaders had worked so hard to persuade other countries to adopt has aroused considerable anti-American sentiment around the globe. If we can't even cooperate peacefully and honestly with Canada, then our foreign relations are on shaky ground indeed, and we are not well-positioned to provide the leadership toward freer markets that the world needs.

Looking Ahead

Many foreigners view the United States with distrust and contempt for our hypocrisy in expecting other countries to open their markets to us while we restrict their access to our markets. To developing countries, this one-sided approach seems like a new form of colonialism.

Our heavy-handed actions are not without negative consequences. Recently, economist David Malpass wrote, "Latin America seems to have decided that the United States is one of the weak links in the global economy. It is reaching out to Europe and China for investment and free-trade agreements, with the view that those are the economic relationships of the future." Similarly, a number of African countries recently have contracted to export their resources to China.

Free Trade Expands

The good news is that, despite the protectionist actions of the United States (and other developed countries) during the last few years, global trade continues to expand. According to the

Settling a WTO Dispute

These approximate periods for each stage of a dispute settlement procedure are target figures—the agreement is flexible. In addition, the countries can settle their dispute themselves at any stage. Totals are also approximate.

World Trade Organization. www.wto.org.

WTO, global exports increased by two-thirds from 2000 to 2005. Too many people around the world have learned that participating in the global economy is the fast track to development for the current momentum toward globalization to stop. If globalization is unstoppable, the United States has a choice: to embrace and promote the process, and through it build partnerships and friendships, or to resist it and so offend and alienate others. In the post-9/11 world, one would think that U.S. leaders would strive to cultivate good will, support and cooperation from other countries.

Former President Bill Clinton spoke wisely when he said that trade "is not sufficient to build a peaceful, free world, but it is absolutely necessary." There is an old maxim that if goods don't cross borders, armies will. More recently, [author] Thomas Friedman has floated a tongue-in-cheek Dell Theory of Conflict Prevention: "No two countries that are both part of a major global supply chain, like Dell's, will ever fight a war against each other as long as they are both part of the same global supply chain." The underlying logic is compelling: If individuals are enjoying reciprocal benefits from trade, they have more incentive to maintain those relationships than to rupture them through war; thus, extensive trade relations are an incentive for peace.

Even if all national trade barriers in the world were removed, there would still be much more work to be done, as Clinton implied, to maximize and optimize the global division of labor. The human race still would have to contend with various attitudes and behaviors that retard economic progress, including: rigid social barriers, such as India's caste system; the indifference of wealthy elites who make no effort to provide opportunities for educational or economic advancement to the poor in their societies; the tendency for criminals and politicians to use coercion to violate the rights of others; self-righteous and apocalyptical religious beliefs; and all forms of bigotry. Viewed in this light, eliminating all government barriers to trade would be only one step toward achieving a complete globalization of the division of labor. Yet this step would be immensely significant. It would lift billions out of poverty, tap into human potential that otherwise would have been lost, and make the world richer due to the consequent emergence of scientists, inventors, entrepreneurs, healers, leaders, artists, visionaries, builders, etc. Surely this is a worthy goal.

Restoring Credibility

A helpful first step in restoring credibility about the United States' commitment to free markets would be to cease filing complaints with WTO and NAFTA panels and to acquiesce with all decisions adjudicated by those panels. In doing so, we might make amends to some whom we have aggrieved, but even more importantly, we would reaffirm the rule of law. When presidents and congressmen lead the way in violating laws that they and their predecessors have enacted, as has been the case with NAFTA and the WTO, this not only conveys to foreigners that the United States is not honorable, it corrodes respect for the law at home, contributing to a demoralized "rules are made to be broken" ethos. A country where the people become accustomed to disregarding laws is on very unstable footing.

In addition, the United States should go beyond the provisions of trade agreements in liberalizing trade. As Dr. Hans Sennholz taught generations of Grove City College economics students, if a foreign government is abusing its citizens by blocking cheaper imports or taxing them to subsidize certain producers, what sense does it make for our government to adopt the attitude, "We will abuse our own citizens until you stop abusing yours"? Making U.S. trade liberalization contingent on other governments instituting similar reforms by adopting the WTO framework was a major strategic error. The best policy for the United States would be to unilaterally abolish all our protectionist measures. This would have three major benefits: It would raise the standard of living; it would promote international peace and friendship; and perhaps most importantly, it would eliminate a whole raft of privileges that go against the fundamental American/biblical principle of equality before the law. Embracing globalization is not only the prudent and profitable choice, it is the right one.

> "U.S. workers and businesses were
> promised . . . a binding settlement
> process. . . . Unfortunately, this system
> is not working as advertised."

The WTO Trade Settlement System Is Broken

Barry Solarz

Barry Solarz is the senior vice president of trade and economic policy at the American Iron and Steel Institute. In the following viewpoint, he considers a number of recent WTO trade decisions as rogue and without basis in established WTO agreements. Solarz argues that these decisions prove the system is broken and should be overturned because they are undermining the credibility of the WTO.

As you read, consider the following questions:

1. In Solarz's opinion, has the WTO leveled the playing field for U.S. companies and reduced the U.S. trade deficit?

2. What was the U.S. trade deficit in 2004, as reported by the author?

Barry Solarz, "Statement of Barry Solarz, American Iron and Steel Institute," Hearing Before the Subcommittee on Trade of the U.S. House of Representatives Committee on Ways and Means, May 17, 2005. Reproduced by permission.

3. What is one example of an unfair WTO decision, according to Solarz?

Despite concerns—particularly with regard to the effect on trade remedy laws and the operation of international dispute settlement mechanisms—American steel producers have supported past trade agreements and market-opening initiatives, including the Uruguay Round Agreements creating the WTO. Indeed, domestic steel producers have long believed in and promoted a strong and vibrant multilateral trading system. . . . U.S. workers and businesses can thrive in a global economy that rewards innovation, hard work and market outcomes. Unfortunately, such outcomes are too often defeated by unfair trade and market distortions that rob the international system of its promise and deny critical benefits to American workers and companies. The fact is that the WTO has not been successful in addressing these problems and, in fact, has often exacerbated them through indefensible dispute settlement decisions and inequitable global rules.

A Troubled System

In 1994, the last full year before the WTO came into existence, the United States had a trade deficit of $150.6 billion. At the time, it was widely hoped that the WTO would level the playing field for U.S. companies, leading to a reduction in the trade deficit. This hope has not been fulfilled. During 2004, the U.S. trade deficit hit an all-time high of $650.8 billion. Indeed, the U.S. trade deficit last year [2004] with China alone was $162.0 billion—a figure greater than our trade deficit with the entire world just a decade ago. Furthermore, the data for the first quarter of 2005 indicate that the United States is currently on pace for a $730 billion trade deficit. These astronomical deficits are not due merely to the explosion of imports, but to relatively poor export performance. Indeed, U.S. exports have lagged since the creation of the WTO, growing only 4.7 percent in the last five years—as compared to a growth rate of more then 30 percent in the five years before the WTO was created. These enormous and unprecedented trade deficits represent a severe imbalance in the global economy that could ultimately have disastrous consequences—including undermining the position of the dollar, destabilizing world economies, destroying the U.S. manufacturing base and damaging the national economic security of the United States.

In fact, exploding trade deficits have coincided with a time of crisis for American manufacturing—which has seen devastating losses in employment and entire industries pick up and move overseas. U.S. manufacturing employment today is down almost 3 million jobs since the summer of 2000. Even as the U.S. economy has expanded in recent years, these lost jobs have not been replaced.

Unbelievably, at a time when the United States is running the largest trade deficits in the history of the world, it has also become the top target of litigation at the WTO. In decision after decision, often based on ridiculous legal reasoning and the invention of new requirements out of whole cloth, WTO dispute settlement panels have struck down U.S. laws and practices—including in areas relating to taxation, appropriations, agricultural support and, perhaps most important, trade remedy laws. So as the United States continues to soak up more and more of the world's exports, our trading partners have seen fit to exploit a blatantly unfair and inept dispute settlement system to extort even more concessions out of the United States—gaining through litigation what they could not secure through negotiation. Americans will not long support a system that operates this way.

There can be no doubt that these developments have already significantly undermined U.S. support for the multilateral trading system. If the fundamental problems facing the system are not rectified, such support will quite possibly disappear altogether.

Settlement System Is Broken

Binding dispute settlement was hailed as one of the central accomplishments of the negotiations that led to the WTO. U.S. workers and businesses were promised that a binding settlement process would force foreign countries to fulfill their commitments to open their markets to U.S. goods—while respecting U.S. laws and practices in critical areas such as the trade remedy statutes. Unfortunately, this system is not working as advertised. Both dispute settlement panels and the WTO Appellate Body ("AB") have issued numerous rogue decisions that have no basis in the WTO agreements. These bodies have also disregarded the proper standard of review in disputes involving trade laws. Finally, these problems are exacerbated by the almost complete lack of transparency in the dispute settlement process. Each of these problems is discussed in more detail below.

Numerous Rogue Decisions

Despite having the most open market in the world and running staggering trade deficits, the United States has found itself the primary target of challenges in the WTO dispute settlement system. Since the beginning of 2001, the United States has been the defendant in 19 of the 36 cases decided by the AB—i.e., in more cases than the rest of the world combined.

These challenges relate to U.S. law and practice in a vast array of economic and policy areas—including tax rules (as reflected in the Foreign Sales Corporation tax case); agriculture (as seen in the cotton decision); appropriations (the so-called "Byrd Amendment" case); foreign policy (as shown in the Helms-Burton/Cuba litigation); the environment and conservation (shrimp/turtles); and morals/decency (Internet gambling). In case after case, panels of international bureaucrats have twisted the meaning of international rules, and invented new obligations, in the course of striking down U.S. laws and practices. These foreign bureaucrats apparently view

What Are Trade Dispute Panels?

Panels are like tribunals. But unlike in a normal tribunal, the panellists are usually chosen in consultation with the countries in dispute. Only if the two sides cannot agree does the WTO director-general appoint them.

Panels consist of three (possibly five) experts from different countries who examine the evidence and decide who is right and who is wrong. The panel's report is passed to the Dispute Settlement Body, which can only reject the report by consensus.

Panellists for each case can be chosen from a permanent list of well-qualified candidates, or from elsewhere. They serve in their individual capacities. They cannot receive instructions from any government.

World Trade Organization. www.wto.org.

it as their province to second guess the sovereign decisions of the U.S. Congress and Executive Branch, and are all too willing to go well beyond the text of WTO agreements to, in effect, make policy for the United States.

WTO Decisions Have Been Harmful

In no area have these decisions been more harmful to Americans—and in particular to our manufacturing base—than those relating to trade remedy laws. The one common thread in all of these cases is that the United States never agreed to the restrictions that have been found on the use of basic fair trade disciplines. Indeed, in many instances, Congress was specifically told (at the time it approved the WTO agreements) that U.S. practice was consistent with the relevant international agreements. These cases have already significantly impacted the effectiveness of U.S. trade remedy laws, and threaten far greater damage if this system is not reformed. Here are a few examples of such decisions:

Disbursement of Antidumping (AD) and Countervailing Duties (CVDs). The AB found that the Continued Dumping and Subsidy Offset Act of 2000 (i.e., the Byrd Amendment) is a "specific action against dumping and subsidization" in violation of the Antidumping Agreement and the Agreement on Subsidies and Countervailing Measures ("SCM Agreement"). The AB reached this decision despite the fact that the Byrd Amendment simply governs how the United States spends the duties that it lawfully collects and does not provide for any action to be taken against dumping or subsidization or against imports that are dumped and subsidized.

Zeroing. The AB has ruled against the United States' use of "zeroing" in a recent AD investigation. The decades-old practice of "zeroing" merely ensures that so-called "negative margins" on fairly traded merchandise in the United States are not improperly used to offset a foreign producer's dumping margins on merchandise sold at less than fair value. To the extent fairly-traded sales were allowed to offset the margins on unfairly-traded merchandise, foreign producers could sell massive quantities of dumped products in the U.S. market to the extreme detriment of U.S. workers and businesses.

Standard for Causing Injury. In several cases, WTO panels and the AB have created a completely new obligation in AD cases pursuant to which injury determinations must "separate and distinguish" the effect of dumped imports from that of every other possible cause of injury. This causation standard—which was simply invented by WTO panels and the AB—is unduly burdensome and likely unattainable.

Facts Available. Several WTO decisions have undermined the ability of investigating authorities to use "facts available" and adverse inferences when foreign producers or exporters fail to cooperate in AD and CVD proceedings, including the five-year "sunset" reviews. These tools are essential to enable such authorities to obtain the information they need to make their determinations.

Safeguards. The AB has struck down every safeguard decision that has ever come before it, and has created such unworkable requirements in this area as to make the Safeguards Agreement essentially a dead letter. The undermining of this remedy makes it all the more critical that antidumping and anti-subsidy provisions see no more weakening whatsoever.

These rogue decisions are without basis in the WTO agreements and should be overturned. Such aggressive judicial activism is causing untold damage to the reputation of the world body and, if unchecked, could entirely undermine support for the WTO in this country.

Proper Standard Disregarded

The repeated abuses at the WTO—and the refusal of dispute settlement panels and the AB to respect the discretion and authority of the U.S. government—are particularly outrageous given that negotiation of a deferential standard of review in trade remedy cases was one of the key U.S. objectives and achievements in the negotiations that created the WTO.

Indeed, the WTO Antidumping Agreement contains specific language stating that when a relevant provision of the Agreement admits to more than one permissible interpretation, WTO dispute settlement panels and the AB shall uphold a member's antidumping measure if it rests upon any of those permissible interpretations. This common-sense provision was designed to ensure that international bureaucrats defer to reasonable agency interpretations and applications of the rules—rather than substituting their own judgment and creating new obligations to which the United States and other Members never agreed.

Unfortunately, the dispute settlement panels and the AB have all but ignored this standard of review. In case after case, they have concluded that there is only one acceptable inter-pretation of the Antidumping Agreement—that imposed by the AB or the panel. This blatant attempt to undermine the ability of U.S. agencies to interpret and apply our laws has further eroded the WTO's credibility, and significantly damaged U.S. interests.

A Lack of Transparency

The defects in the WTO dispute settlement system are only further magnified by its remarkably secretive and non-transparent method of resolving disputes. Among the obvious shortcomings in this system:

- Members of WTO dispute settlement panels are often obscure bureaucrats chosen by the WTO Secretariat—with questionable expertise and without sufficient guarantees of their objectivity.

- All hearings conducted by WTO dispute settlement panels and the AB are closed to the public, which may not even obtain transcripts of such hearings.

- The public has no right of access to the briefs and filings submitted by other countries in WTO dispute settlement proceedings.

- Private parties (including those who originally filed and successfully prosecuted a particular case at the national level, who intimately know the record, and whose interests are directly affected by the outcome of that case) have no right to submit briefs, appear at WTO hearings or participate in WTO proceedings.

No court in America would allow even the most minor legal dispute to be decided by such patently flawed procedures. But the WTO uses them to make critical decisions affecting our sovereignty, decisions that can be worth billions of dollars to U.S. workers and businesses. It is simply unrealistic to expect that Americans—who have long recognized that transparency is absolutely essential to good government—could ever respect or support a body that operates in such a manner.

Periodical Bibliography

Radley Balko   "The Internet Gambling Ban," *Reason*, January 3, 2008.

Daniel Ikenson   "Bad Trade," *National Review*, July 31, 2008.

Daniel Ikenson   "A Trade War Averted," *American Spectator*, April 13, 2007.

Sallie James   "Time to Double Down on Online Gambling," Cato Institute, April 14, 2007. www.cato.org.

Henry Lanman   "Rolling the Dice," *Slate*, November 15, 2006. www.slate.com.

Robert Z. Lawrence   "The United States and the WTO Dispute Settlement System," Council of Foreign Relations, March 2007. www.cfr.org.

Eli Lehrer   "The Risks of Gambling Regulation," *American Spectator*, July 14, 2008.

Andrew Leonard   "One Court to Rule Them All," *Salon*, February 22, 2006. www.salon.com.

Katherine   "Trading Blows," *Reason*, September 17, 2009.
Mangu-Ward

Liz Moyer   "WTO Weighs In on Online Gambling," *Forbes*, July 19, 2006.

Rich Muny   "Why Is the GOP Imploding?" Townhall.com, May 28, 2008.

Viveca Novak   "Investing: How the U.S. Is Getting Beat in Online Gambling," *Time*, November 20, 2005.

Rebecca Rush   "The New Banana Wars," *Counterpunch*, May 26, 2005.

Adam Smith   "Can the U.S. Win Its Bet Against Online Gambling?" *Time*, July 19, 2006.

For Further Discussion

Chapter 1

1. Every county in the world has been affected by the global economic downturn. What role did the WTO play in the crisis? What role can it play in solving it? Cite from the viewpoints written by Pascal Lamy and Public Citizen in your answer.

2. What is the relationship between the WTO and human rights? Do you agree with the viewpoint presented by Amnesty International, which argues that the WTO ignores human rights in favor of its economic agenda? Or do you concur with Susan Ariel Aaronson and Jamie M. Zimmerman, who maintain that the WTO empowers citizens and promotes human rights? Explain your answer, citing from the viewpoints.

3. Food safety is another controversial issue pertaining to the WTO. Harold Meyerson argues that the WTO should use its considerable economic power to influence states to establish food safety standards. Gail Combs counters that WTO does not care about food safety—only its own economic interests. Which point of view do you find more compelling? Why? What should be the responsibilities of the WTO when it comes to food safety?

Chapter 2

1. Peter Allgeier outlines the importance of the WTO to U.S. economic interests while Ernest F. Hollings questions how integral it is to U.S. economic prospects. After reading both viewpoints, how important is the WTO to American economic interests, in your opinion?

2. The Doha Development Round has stalled within the past couple of years. Robert Weissman observes that it is a failure. Daniella Markheim asserts that despite its problems, the Doha Round has great potential and is essential to U.S. economic interests. After reading both viewpoints, do you believe it is within American interests to work to ensure the success of the Doha Round? Why? What can America do to facilitate more agreement?

3. Lori Wallach contends that the WTO is facilitating the devastation of the U.S. manufacturing industry. Daniel Ikenson rejects that argument, stating that the U.S. manufacturing industry is doing quite well. After reading both viewpoints what do you feel is the state of the U.S. manufacturing industry, and how is the WTO impacting it?

Chapter 3

1. In her viewpoint, Margaret Lay asserts that the WTO can help promote environmental protections. Deborah James, however, argues that the WTO is hurting the environment. After reading both viewpoints, what is your opinion on the WTO and the environment?

2. In 1998 the European Union placed a moratorium on genetically modified (GM) food. In his viewpoint, David Moberg defends the moratorium; in a counterpoint, Gregory Conko maintains that lifting the moratorium is the right thing to do. What should be the role of the WTO in such situations, in your opinion?

3. Global poverty has been a persistent and devastating problem. In her viewpoint, Sandra Polaski outlines the ways in which the WTO can help establish food security. Swaminathan S. Anklesaria Aiyar, however, asserts that the WTO's existing food security policies are inherently unfair and are the cause of much of the world's food insecurity. Which viewpoint do you think is more compelling and believable? Why?

4. After reading all the viewpoints in the chapter, which one do you believe represents the best opportunity to improve the WTO? Which suggestion has the most potential and is the most relevant?

Chapter 4

1. The WTO decision on online gambling has generated debate on issues of national sovereignty. In his viewpoint, Joseph Weiler argues that the United States has to follow WTO decisions—even to the detriment of U.S. sovereignty. Countering that view, Phyllis Schafly values U.S. sovereignty above any decision made by an international organization. Once you are familiar with the case, present your opinion on whether the United States should honor the WTO decision. In a larger sense, what is the U.S responsibility to international treaties and international law?

2. Mark W. Hendrickson maintains that the United States should obey WTO trade settlement decisions. Barry Solarz, however, argues that the WTO trade settlement system is broken and needs significant reform. After reading both views, what is your opinion on the WTO settlement system. How can it be improved?

Organizations to Contact

The editors have compiled the following list of organizations concerned with the issues debated in this book. The descriptions are derived from materials provided by the organizations. All have publications or information available for interested readers. The list was compiled on the date of publication of the present volume; the information provided here may change. Be aware that many organizations take several weeks or longer to respond to inquiries, so allow as much time as possible.

Americans for Prosperity (AFP)
1726 M Street NW, 10th Floor, Washington, DC   20036
(866) 730-0150
e-mail: info@afphq.org
Web site: www.americansforprosperity.org

Americans for Prosperity is a conservative advocacy group that aims to educate citizens about economic policy and mobilize people to become active in the public policy process. AFP promotes policies that support limited government and champion the principles of entrepreneurship and fiscal and regulatory restraint. Its educational programs and analyses help policy-makers, the media, and individual citizens understand why policies that promote the American enterprise system are the best method to ensuring prosperity for all Americans. The AFP Web site has a variety of news and information on economic and trade issues, a blog on relevant topics, and offers a regional breakdown of what is happening in specific areas.

Center for Economic and Policy Research (CEPR)
1611 Connecticut Ave. NW, Suite 400, Washington, DC   20009
(202) 293-5380 • fax: (202) 588-1356
e-mail: cepr@cepr.net
Web site: www.cepr.net

The Center for Economic and Policy Research is a research and educational association that aims to disseminate research on economic and social issues and promote constructive debate on pressing problems and policies. One of CEPR's key research interests is globalization and international trade policy, an area in which it provides commentary, opinion, statistical information, and in-depth studies. It also offers transcripts and audio links of important speeches and seminars.

National Economic Council (NEC)
1600 Pennsylvania Ave. NW, Washington, DC   20500
(202) 456-1111 • fax: (202) 456-2461
Web site: www.whitehouse.gov

Part of the Executive Office of the President, the National Economic Council was created to advise the president on U.S. and global economic policy. The NEC has four main responsibilities: to facilitate and coordinate domestic and international economic policy; to offer accurate and valuable economic policy advice for the president; to ensure that policy decisions and programs are consistent with the president's economic goals; and finally, to monitor and enforce implementation of the president's economic policy agenda. On the official White house.gov Web site, students can find press releases, speech transcripts, official statements, position papers, and information on nominations, appointments, and presidential actions on global trade policies.

Office of the U.S. Trade Representative (USTR)
1600 Seventeenth Street NW, Washington, DC   20208
(202) 395-3230
Web site: www.ustr.gov

The Office of the U.S. Trade Representative is tasked with developing and coordinating U.S. international trade, commodity, and direct investment policy and overseeing negotiations with other countries. The U.S. Trade Representative serves as the president's principal trade advisor, negotiator, and spokesperson on trade issues. The USTR works directly on World

Trade Organization issues, disputes, and agreements. It also consults and works with other governmental agencies and the U.S. Congress in order to advocate for U.S. trade interests. The USTR has a number of reports and studies on international and domestic trade issues, including copies and information about the latest multilateral, bilateral, and regional trade agreements.

Public Citizen
1600 Twentieth Street NW, Washington, DC   20009
(202) 588-1000
Web site: www.citizen.org

Public Citizen was founded in 1971 to represent consumer interests in the U.S. Congress, courts, and in the media. One of its key directives is to fight for economic and social fairness in U.S. trade policy, a responsibility of Global Trade Watch (GTW), one of its six divisions. GTW works to ensure the interests of small businesses and the American consumer in the era of globalization. GTW publishes an e-newsletter, action alerts, and news updates on the latest trade policies. It also offers a variety of reports and studies on trade issues and globalization.

Small Business Administration (SBA)
409 Third Street SW, Washington, DC   20416
(800) 827-5722
e-mail: answerdesk@sba.gov
Web site: www.sba.gov

Founded in 1953, the U.S. Small Business Administration was established as an independent agency of the federal government to "aid, counsel, assist and protect the interests of small business concerns, to preserve free competitive enterprise and to maintain and strengthen the overall economy of our nation." The SBA aims to assist all Americans start, build, and grow businesses. It offers a series of free e-newsletters that focus on regional or specific business and trade issues.

U.S. Chamber of Commerce

1615 H Street NW, Washington, DC   20062-2000
(202) 659-6000
Web site: www.uschamber.com

The U.S. Chamber of Commerce is a national business federation representing three million American businesses as well as
state and local chambers and industry associations. The chamber was formed to advance U.S. business interests in the media, the courts, public opinion, and in Washington, D.C. It
also advocates for American interests in international settings,
such as the World Trade Organization. The chamber publishes
weekly commentaries and press releases, and the organization's
Web site offers webcasts and radio clips of chamber meetings,
commentary, and important speeches. The organization also
publishes a weekly small business newsletter as well as the
monthly *Free Enterprise* magazine. The online bookstore offers
various reports and studies for purchase.

U.S. Department of Commerce

1401 Constitution Ave. NW, Washington, DC   20230
(202) 482-2000
Web site: www.commerce.gov

Established in 1903, the U.S. Department of Commerce promotes and facilitates economic growth and American jobs and
opportunities. It advocates for technology, fair and free trade,
increased entrepreneurship, and enhanced economic development. It provides statistical research and analysis for governmental agencies, businesses, and inventors. It publishes fact
sheets, commentary, research studies, statistics, transcripts of
speeches, and the latest economic news that will affect American businesses and trade. The International Trade Administration (ITA) is a part of the U.S. Department of Commerce.
The ITA promotes trade and investment, facilitates the com-
petitiveness of U.S. industry, and monitors compliance with
trade laws and agreements.

U.S. International Trade Commission (USITC)
500 E Street SW, Washington, DC   20436
(202) 205-2000
Web site: www.usitc.gov

The United States International Trade Commission is a federal government agency created to investigate trade matters both domestic and international. The USITC adjudicates intellectual property rights cases and facilitates a rules-based international trading system. It also provides research and information to other federal agencies in order to create an informed and robust U.S. trade policy. Much of that information is provided to the public on the USITC Web site and in various publications. One of these resources available to students is the *Journal of International Commerce and Economics*, which provides in-depth analysis of emerging trade issues. Other publications focus on particular industries, regions, or trade acts.

U.S. Trade and Development Agency (USTDA)
1000 Wilson Blvd., Suite 1600, Arlington, VA   22209
(703) 875-4357 • fax: (703) 875-4009
Web site: www.ustda.gov

The U.S Trade and Development Agency is a government agency that promotes economic growth in developing and middle-income countries through funding and constructive business partnerships, eventually building strong infrastructures and a free trading system. The USTDA also facilitates the export of American products and services to other countries and the creation of U.S. jobs. The agency publishes a quarterly newsletter, *USTDA Update*, which details its recent activities and programs as well as a biweekly e-newsletter. It also publishes a number of position papers, an annual report, and information on public-private partnerships.

World Trade Organization (WTO)
Centre William Rappard, Geneva 21   CH-1211
  Switzerland

41 22 739 51 11 • fax: 41 22 739 42 06
e-mail: enquiries@wto.org
Web site: www.wto.org

Established in 1995, the World Trade Organization is an international organization tasked with the responsibility of negotiating and regulating trade between nations in order to ensure fair global trade in a range of products and services. The WTO works to lower trade barriers between countries, mediates trade disputes, monitors a global trading system, facilitates binding trade agreements, and improve the quality of life for its member countries. The WTO researches and publishes a variety of statistical analysis on international trade, in-depth reports, and studies, such as the *World Trade Report*, an annual publication that examines trading trends and relevant trade issues. Major events, such as seminars and speeches, are Webcast on the WTO Web site and are available for podcast. There is also a special forum for students on the Web site that provides basic and detailed information on the WTO.

Bibliography of Books

Grant D. Aldonas, ed.
Rethinking the Global Trading System: The Next Frontier. Washington, DC: Center for Strategic and International Studies, 2009.

Kern Alexander and Mads Andenas, eds.
The World Trade Organization and Trade in Services. Boston: Nijhoff, 2008.

Kym Anderson and Will Martin, eds.
Agricultural Trade Reform and the Doha Development Agenda. Washington, DC: Palgrave Macmillan, 2006.

John Barton et al.
The Evolution of the Trade Regime: Politics, Law, and the Economics of the GATT and the WTO. Princeton, NJ: Princeton University Press, 2006.

Ross P. Buckley, ed.
The WTO and the Doha Round: The Changing Face of World Trade. London: Kluwer, 2003.

Mary E. Burfisher, ed.
Agricultural Policy Reform in the WTO. New York: Nova Science, 2003.

William J. Davey and John Jackson, eds.
The Future of International Economic Law. Oxford: Oxford University Press, 2008.

Wilfred J. Ethier and Arye L. Hillman, eds.
The WTO and the Political Economy of Trade Policy. Cheltenham, UK: Edward Elgar, 2008.

Hui Feng   *The Politics of China's Accession to the World Trade Organization*. London: Routledge, 2006.

Peter Gallagher, Patrick Low, and Andrew L. Stoler, eds.   *Managing the Challenges of WTO Participation: 45 Case Studies.* Cambridge: Cambridge University Press, 2005.

Henry Gao and Donald Lewis, ed.   *Chinese Participation in the WTO.* London: Cameron May, 2005.

Saman Kelegama, ed.   *South Asia in the WTO.* Los Angeles: Sage, 2007.

Donna Lee and Rorden Wilkinson, eds.   *The WTO After Hong Kong: Progress in, and Prospects for, the Doha Development Agenda.* London: Routledge, 2007.

Rajesh Mehta and J. George, eds.   *Food Safety Regulation Concerns and Trade: A Developing Country Perspective.* Delhi: Macmillan India, 2005.

Richard E. Mshomba   *Africa and the World Trade Organization.* Cambridge: Cambridge University Press, 2009.

Amrita Narlikar   *The World Trade Organization: A Very Short Introduction.* Oxford: Oxford University Press, 2006.

Richard Newfarmer, ed.   *Trade, Doha, and Development: A Window into the Issues.* Washington, DC: World Bank, 2006.

Bernard O'Connor, ed.   *Agriculture in WTO Law.* London: Cameron May, 2005.

Ernst-Ulrich Petersmann, ed. *Reforming the World Trading System: Legitimacy, Efficiency, and Democratic Governance.* Oxford: Oxford University Press, 2005.

Veniana Qalo, ed. *Bilateralism and Development: Emerging Trade Patterns.* London: Cameron May, 2008.

Ronald A. Reis *World Trade Organization.* New York: Chelsea House, 2009.

Gary P. Sampson, ed. *WTO and Global Governance: Future Directions.* New York: United Nations Press, 2008.

Peter Sutherland et al. *The Future of the WTO: Addressing Institutional Challenges in the New Millennium.* Geneva: World Trade Organization, 2004.

Tania Voon *Cultural Products and the World Trade Organization.* New York: Cambridge University Press, 2007.

Harold Whitiker, ed. *The World Trade Organization: Another Round.* New York: Nova Science, 2007.

L. Alan Winters, ed. *The WTO and Poverty and Inequality.* Cheltenham, UK: Edward Elgar, 2007.

Rufus Yerxa and Bruce Wilson, eds. *Key Issues in WTO Dispute Settlement: The First Ten Years.* Cambridge: Cambridge University Press, 2005.

Index

reducing, 23–24, 89, 102, 105, 208
WTO action and, 39
Basic Telecommunications Agreement, 89
Bayer Company, 155
BBC (British Broadcasting Company), 159, 161
Bhagwati, Jagdish, 38
Biodiversity, 144–145
Biofuels, 181–182
Biopiracy, 155–156
Biotechnology rights
biopiracy and, 155–156
compromise over, 153–154
in India, 158–161
patent debates on, 154, 158–159
TRIPS and, 66–69, 76, 152–153
See also Intellectual property rights
Brazil
AIDS and, 43
biofuels and, 182
Dispute Settlement Body and, 60–61
Doha Round negotiations and, 82, 83, 108
TRIPS Agreement and, 152
Breast-milk substitutes, 42
British Broadcasting Corporation (BBC), 159, 161
Bureau of Labor Statistics, 95
Bush, George H.W., 93
Bush, George W. (administration)
affordable drug importation and, 43
annual trade report of, 112
dolphin law changes by, 40, 146

federal deficit under, 94–95
food safety and, 71, 79
global economic crisis and, 53
government regulations and, 170
job outsourcing and, 94–95, 97
manufacturing support from, 125, 127
tariffs by, 205
Byrd, Robert, 205
Byrd Amendment, 205–206, 215
Byrne, David, 165

C

Cambodia, 86, 182
Canada
biotechnology patents and, 151
genetically modified foods and, 168
NAFTA and, 93, 147, 205, 206
U.S. exports to, 90
Carbon emissions, 137–139
Cargill, Incorporated, 76, 145
Caribbean banana farmers, 41
Cartagena Protocol on Biosafety, 146, 170
Carter, Jimmy, 93
Cassidy, Robert B., 71–72, 73
Center for Economic and Policy Research, 110, 117
Center for International Environmental Law, 149
Central American Free Trade Agreement (CAFTA), 143–144, 145–147, 149
Chad, 61
Chamber of Commerce (U.S.), 97, 107